Congressional Odyssey

Congressional Odyssey

The Saga of a Senate Bill

T. R. Reid

W. H. FREEMAN AND COMPANY

San Francisco

Sponsoring Editor: Richard J. Lamb
Project Editor: Pearl C. Vapnek
Copyeditor: Linda Purrington
Designer: Sharon Helen Smith
Production Coordinator: William Murdock
Compositor: Graphic Typesetting Service
Printer and Binder: The Maple-Vail Book Manufacturing Group

Library of Congress Cataloging in Publication Data

Reid, T   R
    Congressional odyssey.

    Includes index.
    1. Legislation—United States. 2. United States.
Congress. I. Title.
JK1067.R44   328.73'077   80-10108
ISBN 0-7167-1171-0
ISBN 0-7167-1172-9 pbk.

Printed in the United States of America

9 8 7 6 5 4 3 2

Almae patris memoriae in amore dedicatus

Contents

Preface

Centuries of literary tradition dictate that the author of an odyssey should invoke the Muse at the beginning of his tale, and I would not presume to ignore that ancient obligation. Although I will not claim that this story about the way Congress works was written at the inspiration of some Olympian deity, I can say that the book was inspired, shaped, and guided to completion by two men who hold the stature of demigods, at least, in the world of journalism: Richard Harwood and Laurence Stern.

The story of how this story came to be written begins at ten o'clock on the morning of January 10, 1977. I remember the time and date precisely because that was a banner day for me. It was my first day on a new job—a job that seemed to me then, and still does now, to be a reporter's dream: covering Congress for the *Washington Post*. My first day at the *Post* began with a meeting of the paper's half-dozen Congressional correspondents to discuss new ways of telling our readers what Congress was up to. Larry Stern, who was then the *Post's* National Editor, brought up an idea: We ought to take a bill, he said, some little-known but important bill, and follow it week by week as it moved along toward passage or defeat. It was almost never entirely clear when Larry was joking and when he was serious, but now he became so animated that it was obvious he had a serious interest in the project he was proposing. "When you got it all done, you'd have almost a film script," he said. "And the name of the movie would be *The Biography of a Bill.*"

For all Larry's excitement, the suggestion was received by the more senior reporters with a total lack of enthusiasm. For one thing, they all had their own ideas for covering the 95th Congress; for another, experience had taught them to be wary when editors proposed long, indefinite projects. "Editors always love these things for the first two weeks," said Spencer Rich, who covered the Senate. "Then they get interested in something else, and the whole project just sort of dies." By the time my five colleagues had all explained that they were far too busy to take on Larry's project, it was evident that I, a new recruit who was hardly in a position to say "no" to the brass, would be elected to write the weekly installments of the *Post's* legislative biography.

From this somewhat inauspicious beginning sprang a journalistic venture that ran for nearly two years in the pages of the *Post* and eventually grew into this book. I must admit that, having heard my colleagues beg off, I embarked on the assignment with some misgivings. They disappeared, though, when Larry Stern and Dick Harwood, who was then the *Post's* senior editor in charge of national affairs, took matters in hand. It was Stern and Harwood who picked the bill that was to be the subject of our biographical endeavor. It seemed a weird choice to me. Waterway user fees? Didn't that bill die in committee every year? As a matter of fact, it always had, but Harwood "had a feeling" that things might be different this time. It was Stern and Harwood who set the tone and style of the series, and it was they who established the scope by drumming into me the lesson that all sorts of institutions outside the Capitol Building have a say in how well a piece of legislation will fare. Finally, they saw to it—and on a daily newspaper, it was no small thing—that the *Post* never did lose interest in the project, even after the bill had been knocked for a loop for the nth time.

Newspaper convention holds that only a reporter gets the by-line, but this is an extremely unfair allocation of credit. Countless people other than this reporter contributed to the newspaper series on the waterway bill and the book that it has spawned. My fellow *Post* reporters Bill Greider, Dick Lyons, Spencer Rich, Mary Russell, and Ward Sinclair were generous with time and tips, as were Shirley Elder, Mike Isikoff, Al Hunt, and Ed O'Brien, who worked for "competing" journals but helped out anyway. A whole deskful of editors, including Dan Balz, Larry Fox, Joel Garreau, Ed Goodpaster, and Peter Milius, managed the not inconsiderable feat of improving the copy without bruising the author's ego. Ben Bradlee gave me an enormous boost by letting me know, in his casual, charming way, that the *Post* was behind me even when I was writing unflattering things about someone with close personal ties to the paper's hierarchy. As the reader of this book will quickly surmise, I had the help of countless "reliable sources" in putting together this story. Sources, you know who you are: thank you.

A whole new cast of editors and advisers helped me when it came time to turn this legislative odyssey into a book. My primary thanks must go to Richard J. Lamb III, Political Science Editor at W. H. Freeman and Company, who oversaw the writing from first word to last with patience and wisdom. Freeman's production staff, including William Murdock, Sharon Smith, and Pearl Vapnek, deserve thanks for turning out the volume at flank speed.

And I must thank my critics. Try as I might, I found it difficult to find tough, critical readers of the manuscript in official Washington; this reflects, I suppose, the Washingtonian's reluctance to aggravate a *Post* reporter. The gap was more than filled, however, by a group of scholars who provided insightful and telling comments on the work in progress—particularly Lawrence Dodd, of the University of Texas, Austin; Jacob Fuchs, of California State University, Hayward; Norman Ornstein, of Catholic University of America; David Rohde, of Michigan State University; and Kenneth Shepsle, of Washington University, St. Louis. Finally, I owe a great debt to Richard Fenno, of the University of Rochester, and the students in his seminar, whose unerring sense of what was right and wrong with my work helped repeatedly along the way.

At home, my father performed a rare service: he read and liked everything I wrote. Peggy McMahon and McMahon T. H. Reid put up with me and the manuscript in cheery fashion—a task far more difficult than writing a book.

It seems completely wrong to end all these happy acknowledgments on a sad note, but I have no choice. I must report that my muse, Larry Stern, fell dead just as the last words of this book were being written. He will never read it, and thus never know how much of himself is in it. *Atque in perpetuam, Mentor, ave atque vale.*

January 1980 T. R. Reid

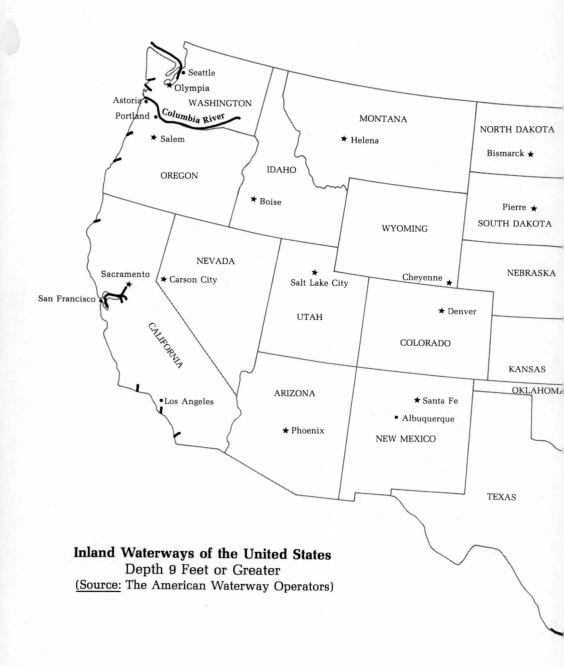

Inland Waterways of the United States
Depth 9 Feet or Greater
(<u>Source:</u> The American Waterway Operators)

MINNESOTA

Minneapolis ★ St. Paul

WISCONSIN

MICHIGAN

MAINE

Augusta ★

Montpelier ★ ★ Portland

NEW YORK

VERMONT NEW HAMPSHIRE

Concord ★

Albany ★ ★ Boston

Hartford MASSACHUSETTS

Providence ★

CONN. R.I.

La Crosse

Milwaukee ★ Madison

IOWA

Dubuque

Davenport

Lansing ★

Detroit

Chicago

INDIANA

OHIO

Buffalo

State Barge Canal

PENNSYLVANIA

Harrisburg

Pittsburgh

New York City

Trenton

NEW JERSEY

Hudson River

Des Moines

Lincoln ★

Keokuk

Hannibal

Springfield ★ Indianapolis

Columbus

Cincinnati

Illinois Waterway

ILLINOIS

Alton

Columbus

WEST VIRGINIA

Baltimore

Washington, D.C.

Annapolis

MARYLAND

DELAWARE

Dover

Topeka ★

Jefferson City

St. Louis ★

Ohio River

Frankfort ★

Louisville

Charleston

Kanawha River

Richmond

VIRGINIA

Cairo

Green River

KENTUCKY

Raleigh ★

MISSOURI

Catoosa

Tulsa ●

Muskogee

ARKANSAS

Cumberland River

Nashville

TENNESSEE

Knoxville

NORTH CAROLINA

Atlantic Intracoastal Waterway

★ Oklahoma City

Fort Smith

Little Rock

Pine Bluff

Arkansas River

Memphis

Tennessee River

Greenville

★ Columbia

SOUTH CAROLINA

Mississippi River

MISSISSIPPI

Warrior River

Birmingham

Atlanta ★

● Dallas

Ouchita River

Jackson ★

Alabama River

Montgomery

ALABAMA

GEORGIA

LOUISIANA

Chattahoochee River

FLORIDA

★ Austin

Baton Rouge

Houston ●

New Orleans

Apalachicola River

Tallahassee ★

St. John's River

Gulf Intracoastal Waterway

Miami

Congressional Odyssey

1

Forever Free?

Anyone who has had the good fortune to visit Washington, D.C., in the spring knows that the capital then takes on the appearance of a greenhouse where the flowers have staged a coup. From the middle of February, when the first saffron crocus pokes up through the snowy mud, to the end of May, when the last scarlet azalea fades away, the city is a blooming rainbow. The traditional center of this urban rainbow has been the Tidal Basin, where delicate cherry blossoms framing the graceful dome of the Jefferson Memorial set the scene for what is, according to the Kodak people, the country's most popular snapshot.

In fact, though, Washington's lushest concentration of vernal blossom can be found on the sloping grounds surrounding the U.S. Capitol. Although members of Congress love to boast about how miserly they can be with public funds, both houses have always spent generously to enhance their own surroundings. The annual budget for upkeep of the Capitol grounds is about $2 million, giving Congress one of the world's most pampered public gardens. The results are spectacular. On Capitol Hill, and in the Botanical Gardens at its foot, the springtime visitor can find hundreds of species of annuals, biennials, and perennials.

In the spring of odd-numbered years, in the first months after a newly elected Congress convenes, the Capitol also blooms with a legislative species of perennial—the tried and true bills that are introduced, year after year, whether or not they have a chance of being enacted into law. Some of these bills, such as the famous one proposing that the marigold be designated the national flower, are introduced mainly for the sake of tradition. "It just wouldn't seem like Congress," explains Senator Howard H. Baker, Jr., a Tennessee Republican who is the marigold's current champion, "if somebody didn't put in a marigold bill." Some perennials have political roots: Congressmen from New York City, where tenants are more numerous than homeowners, invariably introduce bills to give renters the same tax breaks that mortgage payers enjoy. (The bills invariably die in committee.) And some of the never-say-die bills are introduced because their sponsors are convinced that this year, finally, the thing might actually pass. "After all," they would say, "look what old Ed Hebert did."

It was a few months after the Japanese attack on Pearl Harbor when a newly elected Democratic Congressman from Louisiana, F. Edward Hebert, first proposed legislation to give the armed services their own medical school. Nothing came of it at first, but Hebert kept dropping it in the hopper, Congress after Congress. By the 1970s, Congressman Hebert had become Chairman Hebert of the House Armed Services Commitee and, like most chairmen, he had little trouble winning approval for this pet project. Today Hebert's impossible dream, the Medical College of the Armed Forces, stands as a $42-million reality in Bethesda, Maryland.

Beginning in the 1930s, the catalogue of legislative perennials regularly included a short-lived species called a "waterway user charge bill" that set forth a simple proposition: Those who ship freight on the nation's canals and rivers should help the government pay for building and maintaining those waterways.

The legislation was generally launched with a glowing press release pointing out that it would save the government hundreds of millions of dollars and eliminate a fundamental inequity of national transportation policy. Nonetheless, the water-freight industry, which had never paid a penny of tolls or taxes to use the multibillion-dollar network of canals, channels, dams, and locks built by the Army Corps of Engineers, always managed to sink the legislation before it could navigate the first step toward passage.

Prospects were not exactly bright, then, on February 24, 1977, when Pete V. Domenici, a casual, friendly Republican Senator from New Mexico, strolled to the front of the Senate chamber and plopped a waterway user charge bill on the long marble desk there. Not many of Domenici's colleagues noticed the new bill—the 95th Congress was six weeks old, and hundreds of bills had been introduced already—but those who did were surprised. After four years in the Senate, the 44-year-old Domenici had a reputation as a reasonable, realistic sort—not the type given to futile gestures. Why had a practical guy like that latched onto this hopeless case?

Domenici was aware of that sentiment, and it left him sorely frustrated.

"Man, it's so frustrating!" the Senator said a few days after he had introduced his bill. "This is an important issue—we're talking big money here. And anybody with common sense can see that this user charge is way overdue. But nobody around here takes it seriously."

The Senator had a point. To most members of Congress, the waterway fee seemed to be of a piece with the marigold bill and other frivolous forms of perennial legislation. In fact, though, the user-charge bill raised a fundamental question about governmental policy toward one of the oldest industries in the nation's history.

The industry, in fact, was older than the nation. Even before the end of the Revolutionary War, leaders of the nascent United States recognized that a reliable transportation system would be essential to mold the 13 disparate colonies into a single country. In an era before railroads and paved highways, watercourses for barge and boat traffic offered the obvious solution. Between 1800 and 1840, more than 3,000 miles of canals were built, and hundreds of miles more of water highway were created by leveeing large rivers and dredging shallow ones.

For the first half-century of the republic, inland waterway development was left largely to the states, because of a general belief that "internal improvements" were outside the bailiwick of the federal government. Chief Justice John Marshall sank that notion for good in 1824 when he ruled in the steamboat case, *Gibbons* v. *Ogden*, that Congress had "plenary" authority over interstate commerce. Within months, Congress had passed a River and Harbors Act authorizing federal money and manpower—specifically, the Army Corps of Engineers—to construct navigation improvements on the Ohio and Mississippi rivers.

Nearly every Congress thereafter passed at least one Rivers and Harbors Act, and by the beginning of the twentieth century the annual authorization bill for waterway construction and maintenance became one of Capitol Hill's cherished political institutions. It still is today. For Congressmen, winning new water projects for their districts is unassailable evidence that they are working hard in Washington for the folks back home. For the Army, waterway work is a useful public relations tool for staying on the good side of members of Congress. As a result, Congress and the Army Corps of Engineers developed the philosophy that no water project was too big or too expensive to build. This "can do" attitude reached its apogee in the early 1970s, when the Army finished a 30-year, $1.2-billion effort that tranformed the Arkansas River from a muddy gulch into a shimmering blue freightway, creating bustling "international" ports in such prairie towns as Pine Bluff, Arkansas, and Catoosa, Oklahoma—several hundred miles from the nearest ocean.

Congress has been so generous in approving such pork-barrel projects that today there are more than 25,000 miles of inland waterways, which serve as highways for fleets of barges that move huge loads of bulk commodities—grain and soybeans, coal and oil, cement, salt, and chemicals. As the waterway network has grown, the barge industry has expanded with it. At the end of World War II, barges carried about 1 percent of the nation's freight; by the end of the Vietnam War, the barge share had grown to 16 percent. The barge boom did not escape the notice of Wall Street and the major corporations; some of the largest energy, agribusiness, and manufacturing conglomerates have acquired barge lines and found them to be highly profitable subsidiaries.

A major reason for the profitability of the water-freight business is that barge lines have been the only form of transit that pay nothing for their rights of way. Railroads pay for and lay their own track. When the track needs maintenance, the repair work is done, not by the U.S. Army, using federal funds, but by the railroads, with their own money. Truckers move their loads on government-built highways, but the trucks pay for the roads through tolls, license fees, and a federal gasoline tax that is deposited in the Highway Trust Fund, a sort of federal bank account that has paid for the interstate highway system. Air-freight firms pay airport fees and a fuel tax that supports an airport trust fund.

But barge operators paid neither toll nor tax for the damming, dredging, and diking the Corps of Engineers carried out on their behalf. The dollar value of this free service was a matter of dispute; by the late 1970s, the cost ran somewhere between $400 million and $1 billion annually, but it was hard to get agreement on a precise total (like many government figures, the statistic varied depending on the political bias of the statistician). There was no dispute, though, about the commercial impact: While competing modes of transit had to factor in tolls, taxes, construction, and maintenance when setting rates and computing profits, the barge lines enjoyed, on the whole, the lowest rates and the highest profits in the transportation industry.

This unusual federal boon dated back to the birth of the nation, when Congress, in its zeal to encourage interstate transportation, forbade any charge for the use of inland waterways. The policy was enunciated, among other places, in the Northwest Ordinance of 1787, which declared that inland waterways "shall be common highways and forever free . . . without any tax, impost, or duty therefor."

As Congressional declarations go, that policy had a remarkably long life. With a few scattered exceptions, it was 150 years before anyone raised a serious question about the validity of the "forever free" ideal. The question came from Franklin D. Roosevelt, who ordered, in 1938, a detailed study of "the whole subject of taxation upon waterborne commerce." President Roosevelt's panel recommended immediate imposition of a barge tax to pay for waterway construction, but that conclusion sparked a bitter political argument in Congress. Before the smoke cleared, world war had broken out, and Washington shifted its attention to more pressing concerns.

But the idea did not die. Over the next four decades, a dozen more Presidential studies recommended a user charge on the inland waterways. The studies generally found that the "free ride" policy had some positive aspects: it kept shipping rates low, both on the waterways and, through competitive pressure, on rail lines and trucking routes that paralleled the water routes. But that benefit was outweighed, the studies concluded, by considerations of equity, economy, and environment.

Proponents of the waterway fee argued that it was inequitable for the government to provide free facilities for one form of transportation while competing modes had to pay. There was geographic inequity, too; a farmer in western Missouri, for example, who shipped grain to market by rail had to pay higher freight bills than a farmer in eastern Missouri who shipped down the Mississippi by barge.

The economic issue was simple. The federal treasury, the various studies concluded, could not afford to pass out hundreds of millions of dollars in subsidies to profit-making private industry. But the argument went deeper than that. The laws of economics say that any useful goods or services offered at minimal cost will generate infinite demand. Since the services of the Army Corps of Engineers came at no direct cost to the barge interests, the industry's appetite for new projects was never-ending. Economic principle and common sense suggested that, if the barge interests had to pay for the Corps' work, the political pressure for expensive new locks, dams, and canals would diminish.

The environmental argument followed similar lines. Environmentalists, who looked on the Army's battalion of dredgers and dam builders as a scourge upon the earth, hoped that adding a price tag would lead the traditional proponents of waterworks to think twice before asking for new ones.

These arguments had convinced every President from Franklin D. Roosevelt through Gerald R. Ford to ask Congress to impose some form of waterway user charge. But on Capitol Hill, the policy considerations took a back seat to politics. Since there was nothing much to be gained, politically, by taking up this particular cudgel, almost nobody did. There were always one or two lonely souls—mainly members who depended on campaign contributions from railroad interests—who would introduce the perennial bill at the start of each new Congress, but the sponsors generally gave up on the legislation as soon as they introduced it. During the 20 years before Pete V. Domenici got interested in the legislation, only two Senators— Caleb Boggs, a Republican from Delaware, and James L. Buckley, a Republican from New York—really worked on the subject, and neither one made much progress.

This was partly a credit to the lobbying work of the water-freight industry, but it also reflected the fact that "waterway reform" did not strike many Congressmen as a particularly exciting issue. The only members who took much interest in waterway bills were those whose states had major rivers or canals—and they, naturally, were perfectly happy with the policy set forth in the Northwest Ordinance.

Moreover, the members from the waterway states had a great deal of power. By the 95th Congress, when Pete Domenici took over the user-charge idea, coincidences of geography and political longevity had given the barge operators a number of friends in high places —particularly in the U.S. Senate.

Barge traffic moving down the Mississippi, the nation's major water highway, ran through the backyard of James O. Eastland, a Mississippi Democrat who was the senior member of the Senate as well as the chairman of the Judiciary Committee, and of John C. Stennis, another Mississippi Democrat who was chairman of the Armed Services Committee, on its way to New Orleans, home base of Russell B. Long, a Louisiana Democrat who chaired the Finance Committee and was famed for getting his way on just about every bill that mattered to him. Feeding into the Mississippi was the Corps' magnum opus, the Arkansas River waterway, which had brought the blessings of water transit to the home state of John L. McClellan, an Arkansas Democrat and chairman of the Appropriations Committee. The only major freight waterway in the West, the Columbia–Snake River system, snaked through the constituency of two influential Democrats from the state of Washington: Warren G. Magnuson, chairman of the Commerce Committee, and Henry M. (Scoop) Jackson, the Energy Committee chairman.

With senior Democratic firepower like that on its side, the barge industry seemed to have little to fear from Pete Domenici, a first-term member of the minority party who had never successfully sponsored any significant piece of legislation. Even Domenici conceded, shortly after he introduced his user-charge bill, that its chances for passage were exceedingly dim. "Oh, I'd say the odds against me are about 90 to 1," the Senator said. "Of course, a lot of other guys around here will tell you it's more like 900 to 1."

Still, the Senator brought two formidable assets to his uphill fight. First, Domenici's easygoing manner concealed a tenacious determination to succeed at anything he tried; he had an iron will to pass his bill. Second—and more important—Domenici had a strategy.

2

"Get Me a Bill"

Pete V. Domenici inherited his will to succeed from his father, an Italian farmer who had come to the New World in 1906 and opened a tiny fruit stand in Albuquerque. Domenici *padre* worked so hard there that by 1932, when Pete was born, the stand had grown into a wholesale grocery operation. Young Pete helped out around the warehouse now and then, but because the boy had a quick mind and a wicked fast ball, he was encouraged to devote his time to schoolwork and baseball. When he graduated from the University of New Mexico in 1954, Pete signed on with the then Brooklyn Dodgers and donned the uniform of the team's Class D farm club. His fast ball was torrid, but it found the strike zone so rarely that Domenici was out of uniform and into law school, at the University of Denver, within a matter of months.

As a young lawyer back in Albuquerque, Domenici grew interested in a new kind of competition. One day in 1966 he called a dozen friends together for lunch and announced, over dessert, that he was going to run for the city council. "I've never seen so many people agree on something so quickly," he recalled years later. "The whole table stood up and told me I was crazy." But Domenici was determined to succeed. There were 27 candidates that year for three vacant seats; Domenici simply campaigned harder than anyone else, and, when the votes were tallied, he led the ticket. A year later, he was council chairman; three years later, he was the Republican nominee for governor—but he lost the election.

The loss was lucky, in a way, because the Domenicis' eighth child had been born during the campaign, and the family needed a steady income. Pete went back to his law practice and soon found himself representing a widow whose husband had been cut down on the road by a reckless driver. It was the kind of case that should have settled out of court, but at the first negotiating session the driver's insurance denied liability. Domenici, then as now, was a mild-mannered person, but once his temper was ignited it took off like a rocket. And now it took off. "Jesus, that burned me up," the Senator recalled later. "I mean, they were liable as hell, and they were trying to squirm out. I was just—I was absolutely determined, if that case had to go to trial, to beat them bad." He worked six months on the case and, in the end, won his client $150,000 in damages. The case generated a $50,000 attorney's fee, providing a nest egg that let Domenici go back to politics—this time, a race for the U.S. Senate.

For reasons that political scientists have yet to discern, New Mexico's voters seem to favor politicians whose names evoke strong drink. The state's most popular Congressman for years was a fellow named Johnny Walker. In 1972, the Democratic nominee for the Senate was an equally popular chap with an equally evocative name: Jack Daniels. Domenici, the Republican nominee, thus started as the underdog, but he found a key advantage. The Democratic Presidential nominee that year was George McGovern, a liberal whose popularity in conservative New Mexico was nil. Domenici tied Jack Daniels to McGovern early on, and worked tenaciously to keep that linkage in the voters' minds. On Election Day, Domenici became a Senator with 54 percent of the vote.

When Pete Domenici arrived in Washington in January 1973, at the age of 40, it was apparent from the outset that he would not fit the standard Senatorial mold. Most Senators, finely tailored and im-maculately groomed, almost literally shine with the patina of success and celebrity. They look, in a word, like Senators. Domenici, with his wrinkled ready-to-wear suits, horn-rims, and untamed mat of sandy-brown hair, looked like a refugee from a Woody Allen movie who had lost his tour group and wandered by accident onto the Senate floor. Further, the new Senator was an unaffected, down-to-earth type who almost never lapsed into the high-flown rhetoric that his colleagues employed on—and sometimes off—the Senate floor. Even further, Domenici was a practicing Christian, and a serious one. Early in his Senate tenure, he attended one of the periodic prayer breakfasts held for members of Congress in a large Capitol meeting room. To Domenici's surprise, the prayer meeting turned out to be a media event; the Congressmen waited for the television lights to go on before they bowed their heads. Soon thereafter, Domenici quietly started, with three other Senators, a weekly prayer group that met privately in a small Senate office.

As befits an institution that distributes much of its power on the basis of seniority, the U.S. Senate has an elaborate set of rules to determine the precise seniority ranking of each of the 100 Senators. The chief criterion, obviously, is length of Senate service; but to determine ranking among a group of Senators who start their service on the same day, other tests are applied. A new Senator can get "seniority credit" for tenure in the House, or some federal job, or in a state government. Among the 12 newly elected Senators who were sworn in on January 3, 1973, only one had no such credits—Pete V. Domenici. The new member from New Mexico, accordingly, was given the bottom rung on the Senate status ladder, which meant, among other things, that he was last in line when Senators picked their committee assignments. Domenici, who had hoped to land a seat on the Commerce or Banking Committee, ended up on the Committee on Public Works—and to make the blow even harsher, the new Senator from the dryest state in the union was assigned to Public Works' Subcommittee on Water Resources.

It was there, in a conversation with a member of the committee's staff, that Domenici first learned about the barge industry's 200 years of toll-free transit on waterways built with public funds. Almost at once, the concept struck him as wrong. Over the next few years, as he sat through hearing after hearing listening to barge people propose expensive new waterway construction, he grew convinced that some sort of user charge was a must.

But Domenici learned as well on the subcommittee that the barge industry had powerful allies in the Senate. At almost every hearing, a senior Democrat like Eastland, Stennis, Long, or Magnuson would drop by to put in a good word for bigger and better waterway authorizations. It was clear that anyone who hoped to pass a waterway user charge bill would have to devise a strategy to counter that considerable clout.

Which is just what Domenici did.

To win passage of a bill that had powerful enemies, he would link it to a bill that had powerful friends. From his work on the subcommittee, Domenici knew of a perfect vehicle: the user-charge plan would be submitted as an addendum to pending legislation to authorize the rebuilding of Lock and Dam 26.

Lock and Dam 26 was one piece of a major construction effort undertaken in the 1930s by the Army Corps of Engineers to make the northern half of the Mississippi River a reliable barge route. As Huck Finn learned during his raft trip, river people have always considered the Mississippi to be two rivers—"The Upper" and "The Lower"—that meet at St. Louis. As nature built it, the Upper was too shallow for heavy barge traffic. To remedy that, the Corps constructed 29 dams from St. Louis north to Minneapolis, converting the stream into a chain of 29 long lakes, each deep enough for barges up to 9 feet in draft to navigate. The barges cannot, of course, navigate over the dams, so at each dam site the Corps built a lock—a huge water elevator that can lift a nest of barges bearing 30,000 tons of freight gently over the dam and on downstream.

The twenty-sixth lock and dam combination downstream from Minneapolis was at Alton, Illinois, near the confluence of the Mississippi, Illinois, and Missouri rivers—the pivot point of water transit for the entire Midwest. By its thirtieth birthday, in 1968, the lock was in terrible shape. When it was open, it was too small for the modern "jumbo" barge; when it was closed for repairs, which was often, barges and their towboats backed up for miles waiting to get through.

Rebuilding Lock 26, consequently, became the number one item on the barge lines' legislative shopping list. The project had its critics. Railroads, the barge lines' arch competitors, were opposed, and environmental groups, which became an important force in Congressional politics in the early 1970s, were lobbying against almost every major water project. With an estimated price tag of $400 million, the new lock and dam would be the most expensive single barge facility in history, a fact that prompted Senator William Proxmire, the Wisconsin Democrat, to give the proposal his "Golden Fleece Award," a tongue-in-cheek designation that Proxmire reserved for, as he put it, "wild spending ideas that are even more wasteful than the average federal boondoggle."

Nonetheless, political realities made it certain that the new lock and dam would be authorized sooner or later. And it made a great deal of sense for Domenici to use this authorization as the motor that would drive his user-charge bill through Congress.

Logically, the links between the Alton lock and the user charge were just close enough to permit Domenici to merge them into a single bill. Politically, the linkage was precisely right; the very opponents of the user charge were the chief advocates of the new lock and dam. That strategic linkage, Domenici thought, might just permit the perennial seed at last to bear fruit.

Even with that neat political link, Domenici knew, any waterway fee would be a long shot in Congress. He could join the two issues in a single bill, of course, and maybe get a joint user-fee/Lock and Dam 26 bill out of committee. But the barge interests would work hard to unjoin the two provisions on the Senate floor, and, if they succeeded, the waterway fee would be a dead duck. Viewed realistically, the outlook was gloomy. Thus Domenici spent the latter half of 1976 trying to decide whether the prospect was hopeful enough to justify an all-out effort.

"You learn pretty quickly when you get to the Senate," Domenici explained later, "that up here you can be involved in an awful lot of things. So you have to pick something, or a few things, maybe, and concentrate on them if you want to achieve anything. And the more I thought about this waterways business, it kind of evolved as a thing that could be done.

"At that point I had two years left in my first term, and, of course, you never know if you're coming back or not. I knew I was going to run again, though, and it would help if I could go back and say to the Albuquerque paper, or the Santa Fe paper, 'I had enough clout to get a tough bill passed.' And, if I wasn't going to come back, I wanted to have some bill, that I could say, at least, you know, 'Hey, look, here's something Pete Domenici achieved in the Senate.'"

On the other hand, there were definite institutional risks involved in devoting himself to a hopeless cause. "It obviously wasn't going to do me any good among my fellow Senators," Domenici said, "to work my head off on this and then get my ass whipped on the floor by Stennis or Long. So, for a long time, I was scared of this thing. The staff guys kept pushing me, and I was kind of saying, 'You guys, go soak your head.'"

In late summer of 1976, the Water Resources Subcommittee held two weeks of hearings on Lock and Dam 26. The testimony was technical and repetitive; to stave off boredom, Domenici started asking the various witnesses a loaded question: Wouldn't it make sense for the barge industry, rather than the taxpayers, to pay for this new barge facility? To the barge industry, the very suggestion was utter heresy. "It was pretty funny," the Senator recalled later. "Some of those barge guys jumped right out of their skins when I brought it up."

On the last day of the hearings, a barge-line executive who had grown progressively angrier at Domenici's questions could contain himself no longer. "How come you're so interested?" the man shouted from his seat in the audience. "You don't have any waterways in New Mexico. What business is it of yours?"

All of a sudden, Domenici's temper was fully ignited. "Jesus, that got me mad," Domenici recalled later. "In fact, it was that guy, shouting at me, that cemented it in my head, that I would take this on. I was just—I had a combination of violent anger and a burning desire to retort. So I said, 'Mister, you're going to find out what business it is of mine,' and I got up and walked out."

On his way out of the committee room, the infuriated Senator stopped just long enough to snarl at a pair of men seated by the door. "This is screwy," he snapped. "Get me a user-charge bill."

The targets of that snarl, Lee Rawls and Hal Brayman, two staff aides who had worked with Domenici on a variety of issues, were delighted.

Rawls, 34, a lanky blonde who still looked like the Princeton basketball star he once had been, had come to work for Domenici after five years in the Navy. Brayman, 42, was also a Princeton man, but he had spent his spare time there training to become a journalist. He went on to work for several newspapers, developing a feel for politics and the reporter's characteristic attitude of cheery cynicism —attributes he brought along when he joined the staff of the Public Works Committee in 1970.

After working with Domenici since his arrival in Washington, Rawls and Brayman were accustomed to cryptic snarls from the boss. "The Senator is an idea man," Rawls explained. "He's always hitting on some brainstorm he wants to legislate on. He sort of gets this look in his eye, and he says, 'Get me a bill.'"

Typical of the ideas that brought that look to Domenici's eye was a theory of his that air pollution could be reduced if Congress passed a tax on new cars pegged to the amount of pollution each model produced. The two staffers quickly nixed that one—much too complicated, they said—only to see another Senator introduce it, to editorial acclaim, a few months later. Another time, Domenici spent several weeks drafting a bill to phase out federal regulation of trucking rates, but that idea, too, withered under the staff's criticism.

The waterway bill hit more fertile ground. The user charge had been one of Brayman's favorite topics since his days as a reporter, and since his first weeks on the committee staff he had been selling the idea to any Senator who would listen. For most of the 1970s, in fact, Brayman almost singlehandedly had kept the proposal alive—to the extent it lived at all—in the U.S. Senate. It was he who prompted first Boggs and then Buckley to take up the cause, and it was he who first told Pete Domenici about the barge industry's "free ride." Brayman and Rawls saw the Republican from New Mexico as the perfect sponsor for the waterway legislation. Since his state had no barge lines and lots of railroads, the issue was a safe one for him politically. And although Domenici was short on seniority, he was long on negotiating skill and sheer doggedness—qualities that would be essential in propelling any waterway fee through Congress. So when Domenici barked out his angry demand for a user-charge bill, the staffers jumped at the chance.

Once the Senator had resolved to introduce a bill, it was the staff's job to write a bill for him to introduce. This task was relatively easy; like most experienced Congressional aides, Rawls and Brayman could dash off legislative language with the speed and skill of a French chef whipping up a silky meringue. Moreover, once word got around that they were working up a bill, the Domenici team had numerous offers of help. Railroad-industry lobbyists were more than happy to contribute to a bill that would increase costs for a competing mode of transit, and various "public-interest groups," including the major environmental lobbies, sent their experts around to lend a hand.

The substance of the Domenici bill was straightforward. "We talked it over with Domenici a few times, and we agreed pretty quickly on the guts of the thing," Brayman said. "We wanted a bill that would phase in, over ten years, charges that would make the barges pay half the government's cost of building and servicing the waterways."

Laws, however, are written of, by, and for lawyers, and such a simple declarative would never do for the language of the actual legislation. There were no "barges" in the bill Rawls and Brayman wrote; the measure referred instead to "shallow-draft cargo vessels." The phrase "half the government's cost" became, in legislative argot, "50 per centum of the federal navigation-related expenditures." The plan that Brayman described conversationally in 28 words consumed five pages of legalese in the bill itself.

With the user-charge plan translated into the necessary legal verbiage, Rawls and Brayman, in accord with Domenici's basic strategy, stapled to the front of it a copy of the proposed legislation authorizing $400 million for reconstruction of Lock and Dam 26. For good measure, they stapled at the end an extra section creating a "Mississippi River System Council." Such a council was one of the pet programs of Senator John C. Culver, an influential Iowa Democrat, and Domenici thought he might get Culver's vote on the user charge if the council were part of the package.

Rawls then sat down to compose a "Dear Colleague" letter, a form letter to the other 99 Senators detailing the virtues of the new bill and soliciting cosponsors. He had barely begun when Domenici told him not to bother.

"On this one, we really didn't want cosponsors," the Senator explained later. "I was ranking [Republican] on the subcommittee, so I didn't think I'd need help to get a hearing—at least in Public Works. And it was obvious, on something as dicey as this, that we'd have to compromise things away if we wanted to pass a bill. If you've got cosponsors, you have to clear every little change with them."

Further, Domenici knew, if the bill bore only his name, there would be no diminution of the credit if the user charge eventually became law. Finally, there was a chance that, even if he asked, Domenici would find no cosponsors; to woo 99 and win none could be a devastating initial blow.

On the morning of February 24, accordingly, Brayman handed Domenici an untidy sheaf of papers containing the typewritten text of the bill and a fiery speech attesting to its necessity ("Without user charges, the nation's inland waterway system is an irrational anomaly. . . . We are perpetrating the waste of taxpayers' dollars. . . . There is no logical or rational reason for delay"). Brayman knew this "speech" would never be spoken, but the Senator could insert it in the *Congressional Record* as if it had been, and it would serve to explain the bill to *Record* readers—reporters, Congressional staffers, and members—who were unlikely to plow through the complex jargon of the bill itself.

As he carried his brainchild to the marble desk at the front of the Senate chamber, Pete Domenici was already thinking about the rough road ahead. Unless he could make some arrangements, the waterway bill was apt to die a'borning at the hands of a hostile committee chairman.

3

Staying Alive

For a member of Congress, introducing legislation falls into a rare political category: It is a no-lose proposition. By sponsoring a bill that is important to some constituent or pressure group, the member can honestly say that he or she has done the group a favor. But since introducing legislation is essentially a formality, the mere act of introduction, by itself, will not generally stir up any serious animosity from opposing groups. As a result, members tend to introduce bills by the bushel, particularly at the start of each new Congress.

The 95th Congress started in typical fashion, with Senators proposing more than 100 new bills each week. By the time Pete Domenici introduced his combined Lock and Dam 26/user-charge legislation, the bill was assigned the number S.790—meaning it was about the 790th Senate bill proposed in the 95th. (Actually, more than 800 bills had been introduced, because some Senators who put their bills in before Domenici's had asked to have the bills numbered out of sequence—S.999, for example, or S.1313—to get a lucky or distinctive number.) Since the full Senate can rarely act on more than ten bills in a week—and sometimes takes ten weeks to act on one bill—the vast majority of the bills introduced are left to die in committee. Only about 10 percent of the proposals, in fact, proceed as far as a committee hearing. Domenici was worried—and with good reason—that his bill might not even get that far.

The Senate rules set forth which classes of bills will be assigned to each of the various standing committees; on the day a bill is introduced, the Parliamentarian looks it over, decides which category in the rules it fits, and directs it to the appropriate committee. The problem facing Domenici was that this routine process could be disastrous for S.790.

If the waterway fee were considered a tax—which it was, basically, because it would raise revenues for the federal treasury—the rules would place it under the dominion of the Senate's tax-writing arm, the Finance Committee. But Finance was chaired by Russell B. Long, of Louisiana, whose state included two of the world's biggest barge ports and who was, accordingly, an implacable foe of waterway charges in any form. Domenici knew that Long could find several years worth of other bills to consider before he would voluntarily schedule a hearing on S.790. For this reason, Rawls and Brayman had been careful to avoid the word *tax* in writing the bill, employing such terms as *charge* and *fee* instead. But if Domenici's bill dealt with a charge or fee for inland waterway transportation, it would almost surely fall within the ambit of the Committee on Commerce, Science, and Transportation, which had jurisdiction, under the rules, over both "transportation" and "inland waterways (except construction)." The Commerce Committee chairman, Democrat Warren G. Magnuson, of Washington, was perhaps not as harshly disposed toward waterway charges as Long, but he wasn't particularly favorable to the idea, either. Further, the chairman of the appropriate subcommittee of Commerce was none other than Russell B. Long.

From Domenici's standpoint, the most congenial spot for the bill would be his own committee, Environment and Public Works, where the bill would logically go to his own subcommittee, Water Resources. Domenici had a good working relationship with the subcommittee chairman, Democrat Mike Gravel, of Alaska, and he was confident that Gravel would agree to hold hearings on a combined Lock and Dam 26/user-charge proposal. Moreover, only three of Public Works' 15 members were from river states, and Domenici thought he would have a good chance to convince a majority to report his bill favorably to the floor.

Most important, an assignment to Public Works was basic to Domenici's whole strategy for the bill. The Public Works Committee had jurisdiction over waterway construction, so the authorization for the Alton lock would necessarily go to that committee. Unless Domenici could get his user charge to Public Works as well, the effort to keep the two subjects linked in a single bill would fail at the outset.

It was one thing, though, to determine the best committee for the bill to land in; it was something else to arrange for it to land there. Although Domenici had wanted to introduce his bill quickly, he was afraid to do so until he could find a way to steer it to Public Works. Domenici, Rawls, and Brayman spent weeks wrestling with ingenious new interpretations of the Senate rules, but there seemed no way to stretch them enough to bring the user charge to the Public Works Committee.

And then Domenici got an idea.

The Senate's first major item of business in 1977 was a complicated reorganization of its committees, designed to bring a degree of sanity to the crazy-quilt structure of conflicting and overlapping jurisdictions that had grown up over the years. The Senate had more than 30 committees, with more than 170 subcommittees among them. The average Senator was a member of three full committees and 15 subcommittees. This made it difficult to get a quorum for business in any one subcommittee, because at meeting time the members would be scattered all over the Hill at meetings of their other subcommittees. The committee explosion also resulted in multiple studies of the same subjects; at one point in 1975, four different Senate committees were carrying on four different investigations of Medicaid fraud.

By 1976, it was clear that something would have to be done about the committee problem. The leadership responded in typical Senate fashion: it appointed a committee. To chair the "Temporary Select Committee to Study the Senate Committee System," the leaders made an inspired choice—Senator Adlai E. Stevenson III of Illinois, Democrat.

Adlai Stevenson III had gotten into politics the way some people get into a fraternity—on a legacy. He bore the name and face—the resemblance was uncanny—of his father, a distinguished governor, two-time Democratic nominee for President, and Ambassador to the United Nations. When Adlai III got started in Illinois politics, many people thought they were still voting for his father. (Legend has it that when the younger Adlai first mentioned his own political ambitions to Illinois' state Democratic chairman, the chairman offered one piece of advice: "Don't change your name.") By 1974, though, when Adlai III ran for his second term in the Senate, he had become a political figure of his own, and a popular one at that; he won the 1974 election with a plurality bigger than any his father had ever achieved.

Nonetheless, Stevenson, a rational, logical man, never seemed quite at home in the Senate, an institution where the illogical so often prevailed. Of all aspects of the Senate, the committee system was the least logical, and so, when Stevenson was asked to set it straight, he threw himself into the work with a passion. Stevenson finally brought his ambitious blueprint for reorganization to the Senate floor at the start of 1977, where it immediately ran into hostile cross fire from members and pressure groups who stood to lose a favorite committee or subcommittee under the plan. For a while the opposition was so strong that it looked as if Adlai's whole year of work would be voted down. Stevenson was desperate for allies. "To get support for the reorganization," he said later, "I would have agreed to about anything at that point."

Domenici got the idea that Stevenson's willingness to be agreeable offered him the opening he needed on S.790. One afternoon in mid-February, when the reorganization was being debated on the floor, he went loping over to the Senate chambers to engage Stevenson in a "colloquy," as the Senators call it, and thus create some "legislative history" that would circumvent the rules on committee assignments.

Wouldn't it make sense, Domenici asked, if the user-charge legislation were assigned to the Public Works Committee?

"I agree with the Senator from New Mexico," Stevenson quickly replied. "It appears to me that it is logical." He then turned to Senator Howard W. Cannon, a Nevada Democrat who was floor manager of the reorganization plan, and Cannon chimed in as well. "I would agree with the Senators from New Mexico and Illinois. Placing the responsibility in the Committee [on Public Works] . . . is a logical and reasonable approach."

"I thank the Senators for clarifying this point," Domenici said with a grin, and he slipped off the floor to regale Rawls and Brayman with the story of his triumph. But the triumph was less than total. The next day, when the three-way exchange was printed in the *Record*, Brayman took the page over to Murray Zweben, the savvy lawyer who was the Senate Parliamentarian. This colloquy made it evident, Brayman argued, that when Domenici introduced his user-charge bill, it should be assigned to Public Works. Zweben was only half-impressed. Stevenson's concession did make a difference, because the Illinois Democrat was, just then, the Senate's ranking expert on committee jurisdiction. But Zweben knew, too, that Magnuson, the Commerce Committee chairman, might be peeved if a bill dealing with transportation and waterways were routed around Commerce.

Eventually, Zweben decided on a compromise: He would give the Domenici bill a joint assignment, both to Public Works and to Commerce.

It was not the ideal solution, from Domenici's point of view, but it was one he could live with. A bill that has been jointly assigned can get to a final vote on the floor even if only one of the two committees recommends it favorably. For this reason, joint assignment is a time-honored device for skirting a hostile committee. The most famous example, probably, came when the Kennedy Administration had its 1963 public-accommodations civil-rights bills assigned jointly to the liberal, Northern-oriented Commerce Committee as well as to the conservative, Southern-dominated Judiciary Committee that normally had jurisdiction over civil-rights bills. With a joint assignment, Domenici would only need to convince Public Works to approve his legislative package; then he could at least be assured a floor vote, regardless of what Commerce had to say.

Once Brayman had settled the committee question with the Parliamentarian, Domenici at last felt safe in introducing his bill. Sure enough, when he dropped it on the Senate desk on February 24, Zweben had S.790 jointly assigned. Domenici's strategy was proceeding like clockwork. One week later, though, the clock sprung a gear. A new entry—and from an ally—in the user-charge sweepstakes knocked the foundations out from under Domenici's carefully thought-out scenario.

In January 1976—13 months before S.790 was introduced—the Ford Administration, like its predecessors for the previous 40 years, had concluded that some waterway charge should be instituted. In a message to Congress, President Ford promised "quickly" to send a user-charge bill to Capitol Hill. What with one thing and another, Ford didn't get around to submitting his bill until January 19, 1977 —the day before he left office. The White House lobbyists delivered the measure to the Commerce Committee, and, in accordance with protocol, Magnuson, as committee chairman, agreed to introduce the President's bill. (To make sure that no one took the measure to be one he personally favored, Magnuson added the words "By request" after his name on the front page of the legislation.)

Magnuson finally brought the "request" bill to the floor for introduction on March 4. Zweben was not present at that time, and an assistant parliamentarian on duty, unfamiliar with the joint assignment that had been given S.790 a week before, assigned Magnuson's "request" bill to Magnuson's Commerce Committee.

"We started jumping around a little when that happened," Rawls recalled later. "The joint assignment had been acceptable, because that was sort of official recognition that the user charge was in Public Works' jurisdiction. Public Works could go ahead and hold hearings. But with the Administration bill assigned just to Commerce, we were afraid Gravel would decide it wasn't Public Works' business after all. It looked like we couldn't start anything."

In the clubby atmosphere of the Senate, problems like this one are often settled with a casual agreement between members. But Magnuson, a 72-year-old Democratic titan with more than four decades of service in Congress, was not accessible to a casual approach from a junior Republican like Domenici. The Domenici team would have to resolve the dilemma on the staff level. Brayman had some contacts on the Commerce Committee, so he commenced telephone negotiations—and made a surprising discovery.

Although Magnuson and some other Commerce members would probably oppose a waterway charge, the staff director of Commerce's Surface Transportation Subcommittee, Tom Allison, thought the user-charge concept was eminently sensible. At the least, Allison believed, the issue ought to get to the Senate floor for debate. Allison and Brayman worked out an arrangement; they would approach Zweben, the Parliamentarian, and ask to have the Administration's bill assigned jointly, just as S.790 had been. Public Works could then proceed with its hearings, and Commerce would review any user-charge/Lock and Dam 26 package that emerged from the Public Works Committee.

Careful readers of the *Congressional Record* for March 15 might have spotted a minor procedural notation: Mr. Magnuson's bill, previously assigned to the Commerce Committee, would be reassigned, jointly, to Commerce and to Public Works. For the moment, at least, the waterway user charge was still afloat.

4

Clash of Opposites

When Senator Mike Gravel rapped down his gavel on the morning of April 1, 1977, to open the Water Resources Subcommittee's hearings on the combined questions of Lock and Dam 26 and the waterway fee, it was clear to everyone in the packed hearing room that Gravel was less than thrilled about the upcoming session.

The 47-year-old Democrat from Alaska was one of the least poker-faced of politicians. Most members of Congress are masters of the polite fib—they can bring forth a sincere-looking smile and a "How nice to be here," no matter how boring the occasion. Gravel, who had been a taxi driver in New York City before he set off for Alaska, had as much tact as the average Manhattan cabbie—none. He was a real-life version of the classic Humphrey Bogart character: a handsome, hard-bitten, no-nonsense type who didn't mince words. (In 1972, when Gravel wrote a book on major issues facing the nation, the first word of the volume was "Bullshit.")

Gravel's subcommittee had heard testimony on the Alton lock and dam in 1975, and again in 1976. For the chairman, that was more than enough, and he didn't mind saying so. "As I recall," he said, "and this is my third time at this, this whole hearing is just an extension of the last time, which was a déjà vu of the first time. . . . We could beat this to death for 20 years. . . . [A]s an individual human being, I have had it up to here."

Accordingly, Gravel slipped out of the hearing less than 20 min-

, utes after it began. Despite the chairman's lack of interest, however, there was a host of people who considered the subcommittee hearings crucially important.

There was, first of all, the "water-freight industry," a catchall term that covered three major components: (1) the barge lines and their corporate parents, (2) the shipyards and other service industries that catered to the inland fleet, and (3) the major waterway shippers, including coal, oil, and chemical firms, and farmers' organizations. In their various industry associations, the waterway interests had resolved to make an all-out fight to pass the Lock and Dam 26 authorization in the 95th Congress. The Senate hearings would be the first skirmish of their campaign. The waterway people, of course, opposed the user charge as strongly as they favored the lock and dam, but they viewed Domenici's proposal more as a procedural nuisance than as a substantive threat.

"See, that waterway toll gets introduced every year," explained Ron Schrader, a knowledgeable former Congressional staffer who had become the chief lobbyist for the "National Committee on Locks and Dam 26," an organization formed by the barge interests to coordinate their legislative efforts. "It's not going anywhere: Now, if the committee keeps the lock and dam in the same bill with the user charge, we could have a problem, because the whole package is going to get voted down on the floor. So we've got to get a lock and dam bill out of the committee that's separate from Domenici's thing."

The barge lines' chief adversaries, the railroads, also considered the Senate hearing crucial, and they, too, were focusing almost exclusively on Lock and Dam 26. The railroads had formed an ad hoc alliance on the issue with the environmental and economic groups such as the Public Interest Economic Center and the National Taxpayers Union, and they were preparing a three-way attack designed to show that the new lock and dam would be an ecological disaster, an economic boondoggle, and a serious competitive blow to the already ailing rail industry. "Our fight is with the lock and dam," said Bob Bird, a lobbyist for a group of Midwestern railroads. "The waterway fee is fine with us, but it's secondary in our thinking."

Domenici, too, saw the Water Resources Subcommittee's hearings as crucial, but his attention was focused on the user charge. "Most people in the Senate think this bill is some wacky idea that gets introduced every year to keep the railroads happy," Brayman said just before the hearings began. "If we can get the right kind of testimony, and the right coverage of it, we can establish, maybe, that this thing is sensible."

Although the formats of Congressional hearings are as varied as their subject matter, it is usually easy to predict the types of witnesses that will show up at any particular session. There will almost always be a few members of Congress who want to testify, either because of a sincere interest in the topic or because of a political need to appear interested. There will be witnesses representing commercial and political causes that have a direct stake in the measure; just as in a trial, the clash of opposing views from these advocates is supposed to clarify the issues for the decisionmakers. And there will usually be testimony from some objective observers—a scholar, sometimes, or a government official—who are supposed to take a disinterested view of the problem and the proposed solutions. Since these objective witnesses frequently have the most credibility with committee members, their testimony is particularly important in shaping the legislation the committee eventually recommends. Thus, Brayman set out, about three weeks before the hearings began, to find the best possible objective expert to testify on the user-charge issue. Brayman turned the search into a sort of nationwide dragnet, and his quest became the meat of countless wisecracks among his colleagues on the committee's minority (Republican) staff. "Hal's got to find a person who's objective," observed Bailey Guard, the minority staff director, "except the person can't be so objective that he disagrees with Hal."

By the time the hearings convened on April 1—"April Fool— yeah, that's fitting," Gravel groused before the session began—more than 50 witnesses had requested, or been recruited, to testify. The first to appear were half a dozen members of Congress, all from river states, who were unanimous on two points: Lock and Dam 26 should be authorized posthaste, and the authorizing legislation should contain no reference to the waterway charge. This came as no surprise to Domenici. The New Mexican was surprised, though, and pleasantly, by the members' statements on the merits of the user charge itself.

Of the four Senators who testified, the only outright opposition to the concept came from Dewey F. Bartlett, an Oklahoma Republican who pointed out that barge service to Catoosa and other cities in his state might dry up if a fee were charged for moving freight along the Arkansas River waterway. Two others, Stevenson and John C. Danforth, a Republican from Missouri, agreed at least to think about the user-charge idea—as long as it was separated from Lock and Dam 26. The fourth, Charles H. Percy, Stevenson's Republican counterpart from Illinois, offered a ringing endorsement of the idea. "I am absolutely convinced, and have told the barge owners this," Percy announced in his lilting, mellifluous voice, "the free ride is over. . . . To keep up these waterways, the user must pay for the service."

When the Senators had finished their say, the committee called on a white-haired, tweed-suited, bespectacled gentleman who came to the witness table bearing a studious expression and a weighty collection of books and papers. The witness looked, in short, like the kind of man who would play an Ivy League professor in the movies— except that he was precisely that in real life. For this was Brayman's objective expert: Dr. William Vickrey, the McVickar Professor of Political Economy at Columbia University.

Brayman had been bragging to Domenici about this "really great witness" he had discovered, and within minutes the Senator realized what his aide had been talking about. It was evident that Vickrey was one of the nation's leading experts on the economics of freight movement, and it was evident that Vickrey was a firm advocate of user charges on public rights of way.

Reading from a richly polysyllabic statement in his deep, rumbling voice, Vickrey agreed that yes, naturally, a user charge would be an economic boon for the government. But that was not the half of it, he said. The fees would benefit consumers as well—and even the barge operators. These conclusions were obvious, he said, if one recognized that the barge lines' "free ride" gave them an "artificial" rate advantage, leading to "inefficient allocation of [freight] traffic among [transportation] modes." Imposing tolls would tend to make each shipment move by the most efficient mode, reducing the nation's total transportation bill, and thus reducing consumer prices. On the waterways, tolls would eliminate congestion, the professor went on, making it possible that "the total costs of the barge operators, inclusive of tolls, would actually go down rather than up."

The professor's comments were cloaked heavily in academic jargon—he kept talking about "increments in queuing delay" and "the intramarginal residue of costs"—and Domenici felt the need to translate for the benefit of his colleagues. "I am not sure I understood you right," he said at the end of Vickrey's statement. "But were you saying it would be cheaper to consumers if a user charge is imposed?" "Yes," the professor replied, and the Senator beamed with pleasure. Then, just to emphasize that this was an "objective" witness, Domenici posed another question. "Let me establish for the record, you are not employed by the railroads, are you?" Vickrey said he had never been paid for anything by a railroad.

The professor's testimony had left Domenici so obviously elated that Vickrey, as he gathered up his papers to leave the witness table, felt the need to bring the Senator back to the real world, where economic theory so often gave way to practical politics. "I began the thinking on user charges," the professor said in sadder but wiser tones, "when I was an undergraduate at Yale in 1933 or 1934. I have been off and on at it ever since . . . with singularly little consequence, I must say."

Domenici's smile narrowed. "I hope I am not at it that long," the Senator said.

The way was now cleared for the most numerous group of witnesses—the advocates. Their testimony at the Senate hearings marked a kind of milestone in Washington's long courtship with the idea of a waterway fee: the first extended public debate by interested parties on the pros and cons of the idea. The arguments set forth at the hearing would shape Congress' debate over the issue for months—or years, depending on Domenici's success in the 95th Congress—to come.

This was true even though the waterway fee was generally treated as an afterthought. Most witnesses were mainly concerned with Lock and Dam 26. But since nearly everyone who had an opinion on the dam project also had strong views on the user charge, most of the witnesses said a word or three on that subject as well.

The testimony in support of the user charge paralleled the arguments that had been offered in the various Presidential studies over the years. Paramount, of course, was the economic question. The witnesses said—it was Professor Vickrey's argument all over again— that the barge lines' government-funded right of way led to inefficient decisionmaking on inland transportation.

The burden on the taxpayer was a central theme of all those who supported a waterway fee, but none of them seemed entirely certain how great that burden was. Their estimates of how much the government spent on inland waterways each year ranged from $400 million to $750 billion, and suggestions as to how much of that the government might get back from a user charge were all over the map. One point that all agreed on, however, was that this public money was being spent on a private industry that didn't need the help. "Many of the towing companies are subsidiaries of [such firms as] . . . Atlantic Richfield, DuPont, Exxon, Texaco, and Union Carbide," one witness noted. "These companies have no more right to taxpayer handouts than John D. Rockefeller would have had a right to demand dimes from orphans."

The political and environmental arguments were also recited at length. As long as waterways were free to the users, witnesses said, the barge interests would maintain constant political pressure for new waterway construction. But new waterway projects, said a representative from the Izaak Walton League, a conservation group, contribute to "water pollution, loss of wildlife habitat, declining biological productivity, and erosion of recreational opportunities." It was asserted, too, that water transit used more energy than other methods of moving freight.

Much of the testimony in support of the user charge came from railroad people, and their arguments highlighted the commercial struggle that lay at the heart of the debate over S.790. "The railroad industry [is] seriously disadvantaged," said William Dempsey, president of the Association of American Railroads, "by the public subsidies to the commercial waterway industry which is its direct competitor. . . . [T]raffic has been diverted to subsidized waterway competition." The railroads, to be precise, wanted to end a federal policy that was costing them business. The free water policy had been costly to taxpayers, too, the railroaders argued. The subsidy to the barge lines, which drained business away from railroads, was a major reason for the economic troubles railroads had suffered in recent years—and those troubles had prompted Congress to spend billions of dollars to prop up the rail industry. One federal subsidy had forced a second; the taxpayers had to pay coming and going. A witness summarized the situation by quoting Pogo: "You gets to pay double for nothing."

By the time Vickrey and the numerous advocates who supported Domenici's bill had all had their say, they had set forth what might have been, standing alone, a compelling argument in favor of the waterway fee. But of course, the favorable testimony did not stand alone. For every economist, environmentalist, or business person who had testified for the user charge, the waterway interests produced a countervailing expert to testify against. The opponents of S.790 produced an answer to every argument in its behalf—and then they came up with a few original points of their own.

Because so much of the testimony in favor of the user charge had turned on economic principles, the opponents stressed an economic argument of their own. If the barge operators had to pay a waterway fee, the witnesses said, they would necessarily have to increase their shipping rates, which would necessarily increase consumer prices of goods shipped by barge. Economically speaking, then, a Senator who voted for waterway fees would be voting for higher consumer prices for food and fuel.

The higher freight rates would not be restricted to barge transit, either, the witnesses said. They told the committee members about the economic doctrine of the "water-compelled rail rate"—the notion that railroads had to keep their rates down to compete with the barge lines for business. If barge lines had to raise rates because of a user charge, the competitive pressure on railroads and truckers would be eased—resulting in higher rates for every mode of transit.

To counter the environmentalists who had backed Domenici's bill, the barge lines presented an "environmental consultant" of their own, who told the members that waterway construction was actually an ecological boon. "Water transportation creates less air and noise pollution [than trucks or trains]," he argued. As for energy use, the barge interests had research showing that barges moved far more freight with less fuel than any train. Thus a waterway fee would discourage use of the most efficient form of transit—at a time when energy efficiency was a major global concern.

The barge interests pounced with equal force on the suggestions that federal waterway expenditures constituted a "subsidy" to the barge lines and their parent companies. "If you want to see a federal transportation subsidy, take a look at the railroads," one witness said, and he proceeded to lay out, in lavish detail, every governmental benefit to railroads, from the free grants of federal land in the nineteenth century through the Railroad Revitalization Act of 1976, which had authorized $6 billion in federal funds to save railroads on the brink of bankruptcy. As a logical matter, the fact that another mode also received federal largesse had little to do with the free waterway policy; emotionally, though, this was an important point for the water-freight interests. It served to refute the notion that barge lines were taking federal handouts while their competitors made do on their own. To muddy even further the waters swirling around this "subsidy" question, the opponents of the waterway charge all agreed that the annual federal expenditure for waterway work was no greater than $150 million annually.

Domenici had anticipated all these arguments and had armed himself with tables, figures, and quotations from authorities to challenge the barge lines' economics and data. But the opposition also raised some points that seemed to catch the Senator and his staffers unprepared.

The most telling argument was that imposing a waterway fee after

200 years of toll-free transit amounted to—as several witnesses put it—"changing the rules in the middle of the game." The barge lines and the major waterway shippers had made large investments— buying barge fleets and building plants along the waterways—based on the belief that waterways would remain free. Domenici's bill could make those investments turn sour. This was a problem that had bothered even Vickrey, and Domenici was hard pressed to find an answer for a business person who had made a good-faith invest- ment in the expectation that federal policy toward water transit would remain consistent with the past. The best the Senator could do was to promise to look carefully at individual situations where a heavy loss might be incurred under his bill.

Finally, the barge lines brought in a lawyer who argued that Domenici's waterway bill was unconstitutional. The user charge would, after all, raise revenue for the federal government, and the lawyer found a sentence in the Constitution stating that "all bills for raising revenue" had to originate in the House, rather than the Sen- ate. Domenici was perplexed by this argument, as were many of the barge lines themselves. But he managed to find a silver lining in it. "Did you hear that business about the origination of bills?" he asked when the hearings ended. "They must be really worried if they dig up something like that to say."

By the end of the third full day of testimony, four dozen witnesses had uttered millions of words on the questions stemming from Domenici's bill, S.790. But one key group of experts had yet to appear: the representatives of the federal agencies that built the waterways and determined national transportation policy. The wit- nesses from the executive branch would probably have more impact on the bill's future than any of those who had testified already. Accordingly, both friends and foes of the waterway fee were anxious to hear what Jimmy Carter's Administration would have to say.

5

Good News, Bad News

James Earl Carter, Jr., had been President of the United States for
exactly 33 days when S.790 was introduced in the Senate. At that
point, the White House aides and cabinet officers who would settle
questions of policy in the new Administration were still too busy
unpacking boxes and hiring their deputies, assistants, and deputy
assistants to focus on a proposal that involved a fundamental change
in federal transportation policy. On the surface, though, it seemed
simple enough to guess what the Carter Administration's view on the
waterway bill would be.

For one thing, Jimmy Carter himself had demonstrated a noticeable coldness toward the water-freight industry and its allied federal
agency, the Corps of Engineers. That feeling dated back to the early
1970s, when Carter, as governor of Georgia, had been at the center of
a long-running political struggle against the Corps' plan to dam one
of the state's most scenic rivers. The Corps lost twice in that battle:
Carter managed to kill the dam, and he developed a deep suspicion
of the Corps and its waterworks—a suspicion he brought with him
to the White House. Moreover, the newly appointed Secretary of
Transportation, Brock Adams, who would be the Administration's
chief spokesman on transit matters, had publicly supported the concept of waterway charges. And Carter's Budget Director, Bert Lance,
had included in the Administration's first budget proposal a line

item predicting $80 million in revenues in fiscal year 1978 from waterway tolls. Simple logic suggested that an Administration would not forecast revenues from the tolls if it were not prepared to support legislation establishing them.

In fact, though, the Administration's position could not be determined through logical, or simple, deductions. Lance's line item, for example, did not reflect a formal position on the toll legislation. It reflected nothing more than the budgeteer's instinctive urge to beef up "revenues" to offset the ever-increasing list of "expenditures." It was a subterfuge, of course, for Lance to project receipts from a toll system that did not exist, but it was a traditional Washington subterfuge. Previous Administrations, from John F. Kennedy's to Gerald R. Ford's, had been budgeting the same "revenues" for years.

The President's personal skepticism was an equally unsafe predictor of official Administration policy. Whatever Carter's own views on the Corps and its water projects, he knew full well that the inland waterway system was one of Capitol Hill's sacred cows. A new President with a long list of legislative goals might find it wiser to avoid a fight with Congress in this sensitive area. This was the reasoning of Carter's own lobbying team, which recommended that the Administration stay neutral on the user-charge question.

Over at the Department of Transportation, however, Brock Adams had different ideas. The new Secretary, an effusive, superconfident 50-year-old Democrat from Seattle, had been a leader in forging transportation policy during his six terms in the House. Adams had been convinced for years that the barge lines' "free ride" should be ended, but political realities had kept him from pursuing the issue in Congress. Since waterway transit was important to his home state, his constituents and his colleagues in the Washington delegation had pressured him to leave the barge interests alone. In his new cabinet job, Adams thought, he would be free of those political constraints. In fact, however, Adams quickly discovered that the pressures on him as a spokesman for the Administration were at least as great. The executive branch, he found, was much like Congress—full of disparate voices, each with its own constitutency and its own view of waterway matters.

This became clear within a few weeks after Domenici had introduced his bill. The White House sent copies of the proposed legislation to about 20 different federal agencies, asking for their comments so that a uniform Administration position on user charges could be developed. The answers were routed to Adams, and he found them far from uniform. The Environmental Protection Agency (EPA), em-

ploying the same arguments that were offered at the Senate hearing
by the major environmental groups, thought the waterway toll was
an excellent idea. But the Maritime Administration (MARAD),
adopting many of the arguments of the shipping industry, took the
opposite path, stating its view with lyrical alliteration: "MARAD's
position is one of opposition to the imposition of tolls." The Agricul-
ture Department, reflecting the uncertainty major farm groups felt on
the question, wavered between opposition and neutrality. The Army
Engineers sided with MARAD; the President's Office of Management
and Budget (OMB) sided with EPA. The Federal Power Commis-
sion was worried that a user charge would raise shipping rates for
coal. The Transportation Department countered that the absence of a
charge kept shipping rates artificially low.

There was equal confusion on the related question of authorizing
a new Lock and Dam 26. EPA was dead set against the project. The
Army Engineers supported it strongly. OMB thought it was too expensive. The Transportation Department wasn't sure. Within the
White House, the Alton project prompted one of the rare disagreements between Carter and Vice President Walter F. Mondale. As a
Senator from Minnesota, Mondale had backed the new lock and
dam; on campaign stops in the Midwest, Carter had been fuzzy on
the issue, saying the project required "further study."

But "further study" of S.790 was a luxury the Administration
would have little time for. Invitations to testify at the Senate hearings
on the bill arrived at the White House in mid-March, when the executive branch was still far from a consensus. OMB, which serves as
the President's umpire over interdepartmental disputes, promptly
laid down the law: The Department of Transportation and the Army,
as the two agencies most directly concerned with the two halves of
S.790, were to take the lead in forging a single Administration position.

This proved easier than anybody expected. Adams set up a meeting with Clifford Alexander, the feisty, independent-minded lawyer
whom Carter had just appointed Secretary of the Army. Adams had
expected the Army Secretary to put up a vigorous defense of the
Corps' point of view. Instead, Alexander was conciliatory. Alexander, it turned out, knew all about Carter's run-in with the Army
Engineers, and the new Secretary shared the President's suspicion of
the Corps. Thus Alexander said right away that he was willing to
accept Adams' position on the waterway fee, and he asked Adams to
undertake an independent engineering study on the need for a new
lock and dam. Adams was flabbergasted—the Army was asking for

engineering advice!—but he readily agreed to dispatch a team of engineers from his own department to take a fresh look at the Alton situation.

The fresh look took two weeks to complete. As soon as Adams' engineers had reached a conclusion, Elliot Cutler, the OMB staffer who was coordinating the Administration decision on S.790, called representatives of Transportation, Army, and six other agencies to a meeting at the Executive Office Building, next door to the White House. The session was a short one. It soon became clear that Army and Transportation agreed on the two central issues—both supported a user charge, and both agreed with Adams' engineering team that rebuilding of Lock and Dam 26 was not immediately necessary. These views were both satisfactory with the White House, which was anxious to gain the revenues from the user charge and avoid the expenditures necessary for the new lock and dam. Cutler decreed that the Adams–Alexander agreement would be the Administration position. All that remained was to work out the details and send word to Congress.

☆   ☆   ☆

A standing-room-only crowd of barge and railroad executives, lobbyists, reporters, and Congressional aides was packed into the hearing room on the afternoon of May 2 when Brock Adams and his entourage arrived to testify on S.790 before the Water Resources Subcommittee. Even Mike Gravel showed up; after all, he said, "this is a day that might tell us whether Pete Domenici's bill is going to go."

For supporters of the user-charge bill, it was a good news/bad news sort of day. It was good news for Domenici when Adams laid out the Administration's view of the principles involved. "It is no longer in the national interest to continue direct taxpayer support of commercial water transportation," Adams declared. "Water transportation should join the air and highway modes in paying user charges for federally provided rights of way." Discussing the economic question, Adams came up with the highest estimate yet of annual spending on the waterways; he said the figure was "approaching the $1 billion per year level." On the equities of the case, Adams stood foresquare behind Domenici: "It is simply not equitable, not just, that profit-making businesses should have this much of their costs met by the American taxpayer."

The bad news came when the Secretary proposed a method for collecting the user charge. The way to do it, Adams said, would be to impose a federal tax on the diesel oil that fueled the barges. As a practical matter, this was perfectly sensible, because a fuel tax would be much easier to implement than any other fee structure. Politically, though, a fuel tax was the worst possible approach to the waterway fee. Like any new tax plan, a barge fuel tax could not reach the Senate floor without the approval of the Senate's tax-writing arm, the Finance Committee. But Russell Long, the Finance Committee chairman, was a resolute foe of barge fees in any form. Domenici, of course, had carefully kept the word *tax* out of his bill in the hope that this semantic sidestep might keep the bill out of Long's clutches. Now Adams seemed about to scuttle Domenici's evasive ploy. As soon as the Secretary uttered the words "fuel tax," accordingly, Domenici and Gravel raised the alarm. "With respect to the fuel tax," Gravel said, "that would have to go to another committee, the Finance Committee. I serve on that committee. I am very fond of the chairman. I can assure you that the chances of getting a fuel tax out of that committee might be fairly remote."

If the truth were known, Adams was thoroughly aware of the Russell Long problem. During the deliberations within the Administration, he had tried to explain the political drawbacks of the fuel-tax approach. But he had been overruled by Cutler, the hard-charging OMB official who had worked out the details of the Administration's stance on S.790. Cutler had insisted on the fuel tax, partly because it fit Jimmy Carter's general policy of taxing oil products to encourage conservation and partly because Cutler thought Russell Long might be convinced to go along. Brock Adams disagreed, but as a good Administration soldier, he dutifully presented the OMB position as his own before the subcommittee.

The Transportation Secretary was followed to the witness table by another good Administration soldier—this one a real soldier. Major General Ernest Graves, a grave, earnest engineer who was chief of the Corps' construction division, came forward to inform the subcommittee of the Administration's decision that replacement of Lock and Dam 26 should be delayed pending a new study of the facility. It was clearly a message that Graves was not happy to deliver. "I would be less than candid," he observed glumly, "if I did not call the committee's attention to the fact that . . . I testified before the committee last year to go ahead [with the new lock and dam]." In the interim, of course, the voters had given the Corps a new commander-in-chief, and Graves had been forced to come back to the subcommittee and announce that he had new marching orders.

By the time the Administration witnesses had finished their presentations, neither friends nor foes of the waterway fee were quite sure which side had won the day. Adams' forceful language was a plus for the bill in principle, but in practice his advocacy of a fuel tax looked like a real blow to S.790's chances in the Senate. Graves' testimony threw a second monkey wrench into S.790's works; if the Alton project were to be delayed, Domenici would lose the vehicle that was supposed to carry the user charge through Congress. The barge lobbyists, for their part, were pleased about the procedural setback for the user charge, but dismayed about the prospect of more delay on the Alton authorization. And Mike Gravel was livid. The last thing he wanted was another study of the same old project. "If you come back in 18 months," he thundered to Graves, "and we go back through the whole scenario of Lock and Dam 26, this will be my fourth time at it. . . . I think we can study things to infinity." The chairman's gavel fairly smoked as he banged the hearings to a close.

Gravel was still furious the next morning when the Water Resources Subcommittee met to "mark up" S.790. With the hearings completed, the "mark-up" would be the subcommittee's last official session on the bill. A "mark-up" is a kind of brain-storming session in which the members of a committee or subcommittee and their staffers gather around a table with copies of a proposed bill and mark it up with any changes they want to make. When they have the legislation in final form, the members vote on whether or not to send the bill ahead for further consideration. Although mark-up sessions can be crucial—the change of a single phrase, agreed to in a casual exchange around the table, can have an enormous effect on the legal and financial implications of a piece of legislation—they often turn into tedious debates about minor points of terminology. The members of Water Resources apparently thought that would be the case with the S.790 session, because when Gravel called the mark-up to order the only Senators at the table were Gravel and Domenici. The absence of the other five subcommittee members was not a serious problem, however, because at committee sessions, absent Senators can vote by proxy—by giving another member the right to cast their votes. (On the Senate floor, in contrast, a Senator must appear in person to vote.) Gravel held the proxies of the subcommittee's other three Democrats, and Domenici had two Republican proxies.

That made the mark-up process simple. Gravel's main interest was Lock and Dam 26—he wanted the project authorized so he would not have to deal with it in the subcommittee again. Domenici's main interest was the user charge—he wanted legislation linking the charge to the Alton project, with no reference to a fuel tax. In less than half an hour, the subcommittee agreed to report out a package bill that was nearly identical to Domenici's original proposal. All the testimony on the user charge at the hearings had spawned only one signficiant addition to the user-charge title of the bill. To alleviate the problems of small business people who complained about the rules changing in the middle of the game, Domenici added a sentence stating that the fees should be designed so as to avoid "serious economic disruption" for any shipper.

There was a sizable audience on hand for the mark-up, but nobody heard the discussion of the bill. Although the Senate in 1976 had adopted rules requiring that mark-ups be open to the public, neither Domenici nor Gravel liked that idea very much. "Hell," Domenici said, "you can't negotiate in a fishbowl." So the two Senators simply ignored the rule. They huddled quietly with their aides, backs to the audience, talking over the bill in soft tones. When everything was decided, the Senators turned around, Domenici made a single motion incorporating all their agreements, and the "open" mark-up was over.

The subcommittee's marked-up bill went on to the full Public Works Committee, which held its own mark-up on the measure two days later. The full committee session attracted ten Senators, and since the chairman, Democrat Jennings Randolph, a fat but fastidious gentleman from West Virginia, was a stickler for the rules, their discussion was held in public. But there was not much to discuss. Public Works, unlike some Congressional committees, has a tradition of deference by the full committee to subcommittee decisions. Gravel and Domenici had sent a joint letter the day before to each member of the full committee explaining the need for a bill combining the Alton authorization with the user charge. The members were not inclined to argue; they made a few minor changes in S.790 and then voted 14 to 1 (including proxies) to report the bill to the Senate floor.

All these developments were simply too much, too fast for the barge lobby. As late as May 1, the barge interests had still hoped that Public Works would report out a bill authorizing Lock and Dam 26 with no mention of the waterway fee. By May 5, the Administration had backed the fee idea, and the full committee had backed the combination bill that was basic to Domenici's strategy. This left the barge lobbyists facing a painful strategic decision of their own.

Because of S.790's joint referral, Domenici's bill was now sure to get to the Senate floor no matter what happened in the Commerce

Committee. But if Commerce rejected the bill, its chances of floor passage would be almost nil. Some barge lobbyists, accordingly, wanted to tell the industry's friends on Commerce to vote against S.790. But that procedure had a serious flaw: It would kill the waterway fee, all right, but it would also doom Lock and Dam 26. So the lobbyists decided on a different course. They would ask Commerce to report out some form of S.790, and then, when the bill came to the floor, they could lobby for a separation of the lock and dam and the user-charge sections of the bill.

This plan, too, had problems. Under the Congressional budget procedures, any bill requiring federal spending had to be reported out of committee by May 15 so that the budget planners could map the coming year's overall spending goals. The lock and dam authorization, of course, involved spending, but there clearly was not enough time before May 15 for the Commerce Committee to hold hearings and report its own version of S.790. So the barge lines had to ask Warren Magnuson, Commerce's chairman, to waive hearings and agree to an immediate full committee mark-up of the bill. Magnuson was not at all happy with this shortcut procedure, but he finally consented to schedule a mark-up on May 12—three days before the deadline.

Because of the haste, the Commerce Committee's mark-up was something less than a model of responsible legislating. Since hardly any of the committee members had had time to read S.790, they had to mark it up in almost total ignorance of its provisions. To get around this difficulty, Magnuson undertook to explain the bill to the committee at the start of the session. About a third of the way through, though, the 72-year-old chairman lost his train of thought, and the explanation trailed off into small talk. That didn't stop the members from debating the bill, however. Most were strongly opposed to the user charge, but they realized they would have to send some version of S.790 to the floor. To deal with this dilemma, Long proposed new language calling for immediate authorization of Lock and Dam 26 but putting off any action on user charges for at least 18 months, pending a new study of the issue. This proposal, which a group of barge lobbyists had drafted and presented to Long, was a perfect solution from the viewpoint of the water-freight industry. It would get work under way at Alton and push the waterway charge, for a while, at least, off to the side. Thus the Long version of the bill was approved by a strong majority.

Once this basic approach was settled, the committee members offered a flurry of amendments to the bill, and amendments to those amendments, so that by the end of the session nobody was certain exactly what the Commerce version of the legislation would include. "Without objection," Magnuson said, "we'll let the staff clean all this up and put together a bill." Nobody objected. S.790 had emerged, wounded but still alive, from its second committee.

Among the spectators at the Commerce Committee mark-up was Hal Brayman, and when the result was obvious he went racing back to Domenici's office with the news. The Senator heard him out with a mixture of pride and concern. The basic strategy, the linkage between the user charge and the Alton project, had worked beautifully; without it, both men agreed, S.790 would have died in one or both of the committees that considered it. The future, though, looked less promising. There was no doubt that opponents of the waterway fee would do everything they could to break Domenici's strategic link when S.790 reached the Senate floor. Commerce's version of the bill would give them an easy way to do just that.

If S.790 were to go any further, the Senator and the staffer agreed, they would have to find some way to keep the bill's essential linkage alive.

6

A Friend in Need

Ever since Pete Domenici first came up with the idea of linking his user-charge proposal with the authorization for Lock and Dam 26, Brayman and Rawls had talked about this strategy as "the hostage plan." The theory was that some Senators who would never vote for a user charge under ordinary circumstances would have to vote for S.790 to free the "hostage"—the lock and dam. Domenici disliked that terminology, partly because it seemed a little violent for his taste and partly because he knew that, as a relatively obscure junior member of the minority party, he did not have enough institutional power in the Senate to hold any bill "hostage" on the floor against the will of senior members like Long, Magnuson, and McClellan. On the other hand, Domenici knew someone who did have the necessary power: Jimmy Carter.

Actually, Domenici hardly "knew" the new President at all. They had met a few times, as politicians do, across the receiving lines of huge official receptions; on those occasions, the President called the Senator "Peter," a name Domenici never used. But Domenici did have a good personal relationship with somebody close to Carter on the user-charge issue: Brock Adams. In 1974, when the two houses of Congress had each established a new committee to review the federal budget, Adams had been one of the charter members on the House side, and Domenici in the Senate. They had shared a sense of pioneer camaraderie, and had discovered, in House–Senate conferences, that they worked well together. In one of those "odd couple" relationships that pop up now and again on Capitol Hill, the liberal Democratic Congressman from Seattle and the conservative Republican Senator from Albuquerque became good friends. When Adams left Congress to join Carter's cabinet, the two men kept in touch; Domenici called Adams regularly to brief him on the latest budget developments.

Because S.790, Domenici's chief legislative interest that spring, came within Adams' bailiwick at Transportation, the bill became another regular topic of conversation between the two men. Domenici told Adams from the outset about the hostage strategy. It was obvious to both men that Adams, speaking for the President, could give that strategy real force. "I told Brock," Domenici recalled later, "that the connection between the lock and the user fee was pretty fragile if Pete Domenici was the only person linking the two. But if Jimmy Carter says that he won't go along with Lock 26 unless there's a user-charge bill on it—then you're talking pretty strong linkage."

Domenici said, too, that a vague exhortation from the executive branch would not be sufficient. What was needed, to assure that Lock and Dam 26 and the waterway fee would not be separated on the Senate floor, was an explicit threat: Carter would veto any authorization for the Alton lock unless a user charge was part of the same bill.

Adams was receptive. Domenici's thinking made sense, the Secretary later explained, and it made sense for the Administration to go along with him. It was time for the nation to bite the bullet on the waterway-fee principle, he thought; he knew that Bert Lance, the Budget Director, would agree on that point, because the principle would save the government money. Further, the user charge was a good issue for Adams personally. If Brock Adams' Transportation Department could have a hand in finally winning this perennial battle, it would enhance his status on Capitol Hill—and that would help him when he brought other transportation issues to Congress. And a victory—or even a close defeat—would win him the respect and confidence of the President and the White House staff.

Normally, of course, a newly appointed cabinet member could expect to have the confidence of the President who had appointed him, but this was not true in Adams' case. Carter had appointed Adams to Transportation largely because of pressure from Adams' friends on Capitol Hill. So Adams got the job, but he also earned the resentment and distrust of the White House staff.

In addition to these personal considerations, Adams kept hearing about the waterway bill from his own staff—or, at least, from one member of it, Susan Williams, an outgoing young woman Adams had hired to run his lobbying operation. In the first months of 1977, Williams was frankly depressed with her new job. "The guy I took over from had been a deputy assistant secretary," she recalled later, "which is a good title and it means a good salary. But when I came in to do the same work, they gave me a lot lower pay and no title. See, they'd never had a woman in that job before. They treated me like a typist."

To make matters worse, Williams had trouble getting interested in the routine highway and airport bills for which she was responsible. But the waterway bill was different. "I just fell in love with that thing," Williams said. "I mean, here I had a chance to work on something that would really make history if it passed. Of course, the chances weren't too good that it would, but anyway, every time I saw Brock, I would talk to him about that bill. I kept saying, 'Brock, this is a great issue.' And I knew Domenici was working on Brock, too, and finally one day Brock said I could put it on my action list and get to work."

Still, Adams was not certain that he could commit Carter to threaten a veto of the Alton project to help Domenici pass his user charge. A veto was big medicine—not the kind of thing a President would throw around to win unimportant battles. And a Presidential veto of a water construction project, a field that Congress considered its own prerogative, would almost surely spawn sour relations between the White House and Capitol Hill.

Late in April, Adams called Carter to discuss the matter. "I was surprised," the Secretary recalled afterward, "by how well versed he was on the user-charge concept. I didn't have to brief him at all. He made it clear that he thought the Corps was sometimes excessive in proposing new projects, and this might be a way to curb that. There was no question that he favored a user charge."

The only question was whether Carter felt strongly enough about the user charge to threaten a veto in order to get it. The President was not yet ready to decide that; he told Adams to go over the pros and cons with Stuart Eizenstat, the domestic policy expert on the White House staff.

By May 2, when Adams testified before the subcommittee, the White House had not yet decided whether it would support Domenici's hostage plan. Domenici, when it came his turn to question Adams at the hearing, pressed the point. Was it fair to assume, Domenici asked, that the Administration felt "there is a relationship between rebuilding Lock and Dam 26 and the imposition or the taking of action to enact [user charges]?"

Adams paused for a long minute—and then dove right in. "Your statement is accurate," he said at last. Barring some emergency, the Secretary said, "I think that any construction there should be tied to waterway user charges."

That answer was a spur-of-the-moment decision on Adams' part, and it went further than he had authority to go. But it stood him in good stead a week later, when the Secretary and two of his aides traveled to the White House for a meeting with Eizenstat and various junior White House staffers. Eizenstat and his aides said they were all for the user charge, but they were reluctant to threaten a veto. To Eizenstat, the issue was simply not important enough to put the President's personal prestige on the line. Maybe, he said, Domenici could pass his bill without Carter's help. Adams responded that the linkage between the two issues had already been acknowledged by the Administration—in his own testimony. A veto threat would be a logical extension of what Adams had already told the subcommittee.

Eizenstat closed the meeting by promising to talk to the President about the problem. For two weeks, Adams heard nothing. Then, a few days after the two Senate committees had reported S.790, Eizenstat called. Carter, he said, had sided with Adams. The issue was worthy of direct Presidential action, Carter had decided, and Adams was free to tell Congress that any authorization bill for the Alton project would be vetoed unless the user charge were approved along with it. As soon as Adams hung up, he picked up the telephone again to pass the word to Domenici.

Domenici was delighted, of course, but his first fear was that Adams' veto letter would arrive too late to do any good. A floor vote on S.790 was due any time now; what if the bill came up before the veto letter had circulated? To avoid that calamity, Domenici's aide Lee Rawls went racing off to see William Hildenbrand, the aide who represented the Republicans in negotiations over the scheduling of Senate business. "I don't care how you do it," Rawls said, "but you've got to get that S.790 vote put off." "No problem," Hildenbrand replied. Hildenbrand had a working relationship with his counterparts on the Democratic staff that permitted either side to delay scheduling of most bills. So it was no problem, in fact, to arrange that the waterway bill would not come to the floor until the middle of June.

On May 20, Brock Adams dispatched a letter to the Democratic and Republican leadership of the Senate. It did not mince words. "Because of the importance of this legislation to overall transportation planning," it said, "and because of its impact on the President's effort to balance the budget, I feel I should inform you and the Senate of the President's very firm intention to veto any bill authorizing construction of a new Lock and Dam 26 . . . which does not also contain a provision for the establishment of waterway user charges."

Within hours after the letter's arrival on Capitol Hill, a friendly Senator had passed a copy on to Harry Cook, the director of the Washington office of the National Waterways Conference, an important water-freight industry group. Cook immediately convened a meeting of barge lobbyists to consider this new problem. The mood at this gathering was one of concern, but not of panic. Previously, the barge lines had considered Domenici's strategy a minor procedural nuisance, easy to defeat on the Senate floor. With Jimmy Carter on board, the "hostage" plan became a more formidable obstacle—but not, as the barge lines saw it, an insurmountable one.

A few days after the meeting, Cook, a small, wiry man who had never lost the friendly drawl of his native Alabama, summarized the consensus view. "We think the President has made a pretty bad mistake," Cook said. "Senator Domenici knows he doesn't have the votes to pass a user charge—otherwise, he'd just bring his bill to the floor without all this fancy strategy. We know we've got the votes to pass an authorization for Lock and Dam 26, and we've got the votes to override a veto, if we have to. So if the President holds firm on this veto business, he's going to take a beating on this bill."

7

The Lamb

One of the skills essential to success as a Washington lobbyist is a mastery of the art of "counting heads"—surveying members of Congress to find out how they are likely to vote on a particular bill in committee or on the floor. An accurate "head count" can be extremely valuable in planning the timing and focus of a lobbying campaign —but accuracy in this iffy business is a sometime thing. One member will refuse to commit himself ahead of time; another, moved by the politican's instinctive urge to tell people what they want to hear, will promise both supporters and opponents of a measure that he or she is on their side. Thus it is not at all uncommon to hear two lobbyists, on opposite sides of a given bill, both predicting with near certainty that they have the votes to win.

During the first few months of S.790's life, however, there were no such disagreements. Head counts taken by both sides showed that Domenici's bill was going to lose by a substantial margin. Then came the Administration's veto letter. Two weeks after the letter arrived on Capitol Hill, the head counters noticed that some earlier opponents of the user charge were taking a second look. If Carter meant what he said—if it really would take a vote for the user charge to get a new Lock and Dam 26—some Senators might go along. Others, however, felt the veto threat was a bluff. Nonetheless, by the second week of June, Sue Williams reported to her boss, Adams, that the Senate was

44

split about 40 to 40 on the user charge, with 20 members undecided. Although hardly a portent of sure victory, this was by far the most optimistic assessment ever of the user charge's chances, and it came as electrifying news to Domenici and his aides. "You can't really trust those head counts," Brayman said, struggling unsuccessfully to remain calm, "but if that's anywhere near right, we're in good shape!"

With prospects brightening in the Senate, Domenici turned to a rather fundamental problem he had ignored all spring: There was another house of Congress to deal with. Even if Domenici were to eke out a victory on the Senate floor, all his efforts would be futile if the barge bill came to a halt in the House of Representatives. And it looked as if that might happen. A user-charge bill, designated H.R.4339, had been introduced in the House a few days after Domenici had put in S.790 on the Senate side. But the House bill was making less forward progress than a barge on a sandbar.

The sponsor of H.R.4339 was Berkley Bedell, a gentle soul from Spirit Lake, Iowa, who represented the rural northwest corner of that state in Congress. Bedell, a soft-spoken, low-keyed 56-year-old Democrat, was sort of a lamb among lions in Congress. He was just not the type to pressure his waterway bill, or anything else, past hostile committee leaders. "I don't usually call the chairman or cajole people or things like that," he said a few weeks after he had dropped H.R.4339 into the hopper. "I don't really think I can force anybody to get going on that bill."

Still, Bedell had a knack, in his quiet way, for getting things done. As a high school student in Spirit Lake during the Depression, Bedell had learned to braid dog's hair around old fishhooks and sell the results as trout flies to make spending money. He kept at it after graduation and gradually built his pastime into a fishing-tackle firm, Berkley and Company, with 800 employees and $20 million in annual sales. By his fiftieth birthday, the business was booming, Bedell was a millionaire, and he decided to take a stab at politics. With the same industry he had brought to the production of fishing gear, he set out in 1971 to win a seat in Congress. He lost in 1972 to Wiley Mayne, a solidly entrenched Republican incumbent, but never stopped running. In a rematch against Mayne in 1974, Bedell took 55 percent of the vote. He packed up his family and his favorite graphite rod and set out for Washington.

Bedell was a firm believer in the concept of representative democracy, and he was determined to be the "Representative" of Iowa's 6th Congressional district in fact as well as in title. So he established a regular circuit of what he called "open-door meetings"—at least two a year in each of the district's 22 counties—in which his constituents would make motions and cast votes to determine two things: which issues Bedell should concentrate on in Congress and how he should vote on pending bills. It was in these sessions that Bedell first heard about the billions of dollars worth of right-of-way that commercial barge lines were receiving for free from the government. In Monona County, in Osceola, in Winnebago the subject came up, and the people asked their Congressman to do something about it.

"I never knew much about this," Bedell explained later. "But at these meetings people kept saying it wasn't fair. The railroads had to pay for their track bed; truckers paid into a fund for highways. Why should the barges go free?" It was not just an abstract notion of fairness, however, that motivated Bedell's constituents. Most of the farmers in his corner of Iowa shipped their grain to market by rail, and they paid higher freight rates than eastern Iowans, who shipped by barge down the Mississippi. In effect, their federal taxes were subsidizing the operations of their competitors in the eastern part of the state.

When Bedell came back to Washington after the 1976 election (he had been reelected with 68 percent of the vote), he asked his legislative assistant, Bill Endicott, to put together a waterway user charge bill. Endicott, who was fairly new on the job, knew little about drafting legislation and even less about the barge industry. He took the problem to Ward Hussey, a cheery veteran of 30 years' service in the House's Office of Legislative Counsel, a nest of lawyers who help Congressmen turn their vague ideas into specific statutory language. For Hussey, who had drafted the Internal Revenue Code and scores of other complex bills, a little thing like a waterway toll was a piece of cake. He borrowed some language from previous versions of the perennial bill, threw in some standard conditions and exemptions, and ground out H.R.4339 in a few days. With the bill in hand, Endicott sent out a "Dear Colleague" letter, over Bedell's signature, seeking cosponsors. Ten signed on, and Bedell dropped his bill in the hopper.

But there it stopped. Bedell's bill was referred jointly to the Public Works Committee and to the Committee on Ways and Means, the House's tax-writing arm. Senior members of both committees had close ties with the water-freight industry; a waterway fee was unlikely to find favor in either one. This problem, of course, was not unlike the one that had faced S.790 in the Senate. But in the House, such institutional obstacles are more difficult to overcome. Because of the fragmentation of power among 435 members, it is much harder in the

House for a single member to get anywhere with an idea that is unpalatable to the leadership. In the Senate, it is not uncommon for a junior member, even in the minority party, to steer a personal bill through to passage. In the House, such an achievement is almost unheard of. The most common way for a junior Congressman to pass a pet piece of legislation is to persuade a committee or subcommittee chairman to adopt it as his own and take it to the floor in his name. Bedell, of course, had little hope of convincing the heads of the appropriate House committees to adopt the waterway fee. H.R.4339 was likely to remain Berkley Bedell's own bill—which meant it was not going to go very far.

Thus when Domenici asked his staffers to find out what was happening to the waterway bill on the House side, they came back with a bleak prognosis. "Some guy from Iowa has a bill in," Brayman reported, "but he'll never even get it to the floor." Domenici's Mission Impossible, then, was to find a means, from his seat in the Senate, to force his idea through the other half of Congress. The Senator stewed over the problem for some time and eventually decided to approach that mission through a conference committee.

The Constitution requires that legislation must be approved by both Houses of Congress before it can be signed into law by the President. Sometimes—particularly on minor bills—that requirement is simple to meet: both House and Senate pass a measure in identical form and send it to the White House. On major legislation, however, it is more common for the two bodies to produce two different versions. To mold these differing bills into a single, jointly acceptable piece of legislation, both versions are sent to a "conference committee," with membership drawn from both houses. The conferees generally do their work through compromise: each house yields partly to the other, and the final conference version contains pieces of both the House and the Senate bill. The conferees' final version of the bill must then be approved in each house, but that is normally a formality.

The possibility of a compromise in conference provided Domenici the opening he needed. If he could pass S.790 on the Senate floor, he would try to attach that bill to some other piece of legislation—one that had already passed in the House. When this legislative vehicle went to conference, Domenici could insist that the House conferees accept the user-charge/Lock and Dam 26 provision. If they did, the user charge could go to the House floor as part of the conference bill.

This conference-committee approach, then, would bring the user charge before the full House even if Bedell's bill were still moldering in a subcommittee. To make it work, though, Domenici would need the right vehicle—a bill to carry S.790 to a conference. The choice was easy: He picked the Omnibus Water Resources Bill, a compendium of two dozen or so pork-barrel public-works projects that had been collected, for administrative convenience, into a single legislative package. The House had already passed its version of the omnibus bill—designated H.R.5885—and the Senate was sure to follow suit. Since it was a waterway authorization bill, it would be a perfectly logical place to append a waterway charge. Moreover, the omnibus bill was a product of the Senate Public Works Committee. That meant that the Senate conferees on the bill would be chosen from Public Works' members—who had already approved the user-charge concept by a healthy margin. Domenici himself, as a member of Public Works, would likely be a conferee, meaning he would be on hand personally to push for the user charge in conference.

Domenici concluded, then, that if he could get the Senate to approve S.790, he would try to attach it to the omnibus bill. On that vehicle, the waterway user charge might just ride through the House.

It was a neat solution, but there was one overriding problem: Domenici might never get a chance to try it. The whole plan would go up in smoke if S.790 were defeated on the Senate floor. And that still seemed likely. Even with the veto letter, it was not clear that the hostage strategy—the linkage of Lock and Dam 26 and the user charge—would work. Some Senators, believing that Carter's veto threat was a bluff, were still determined to separate the two issues on the floor. Moreover, the Administration's involvement, together with media coverage of the bill, had focused more attention on the user-charge issue than it had ever received before. That, in turn, had provoked advocates on both sides to step up their efforts. By the middle of June, the waterway user charge was the focus of a battle royal between two well-funded lobbying armies.

8

A Laundry
and Two Big Fish

When Pete Domenici heard the names of those who had registered to lobby on S.790, it sounded at first as if the debate on his bill would involve a bunch of good-government types carrying on a philosophical discussion about public policy. Among those supporting the user-charge legislation were such pristine-sounding groups as the Environmental Policy Center, the Coalition for American Rivers, the Council for a Sound Waterways Policy, and the Public Interest Economics Center. Those arrayed on the opposing side included the Association for the Improvement of the Mississippi River, the Upper Mississippi River Valley Association, and a passel of former Congressmen, Senators, and executive branch officials.

In fact, as Domenici gradually discovered, the efforts of all those organizations and officials were orchestrated and financed by the two major commercial combatants in the lobbying war: the railroad industry, fighting for the imposition of tolls, and the barge lines, fighting against them. There were a few independent voices in the debate for and against S.790, but they were dwarfed by the money and manpower deployed for battle by the two interests with a major financial stake in the legislation.

Commander-in-chief of the allied forces lobbying for the waterway toll was J. D. Feeney, a genial ("Call me Joe") 53-year-old bundle of energy who was General Counsel of the Western Railroads Association, a Chicago-based organization of 22 railroads operating in the Mississippi Valley. Feeney had inherited the user-charge fight more or less by default. He had been leading the railroads' campaign against the Lock and Dam 26 authorization for years, and when Domenici linked the user-charge issue with the lock and dam, Feeney's lobbying organization took up that issue as well. As soon as Feeney began to plan his campaign, he found himself up against a ticklish tactical problem. The railroads, as the chief competitors of the barge industry, were naturally suspect when they lobbied on barge issues. To give his operation a degree of credibility, Feeney wanted to enlist some allies who had no financial interest in the legislation. "I knew there were environmentalists and other people out there who agreed with us," Feeney explained later. "They thought the lock and dam would be a disaster and the user charges would be great. So obviously we wanted these people to be active in the lobbying. But these guys were getting along on baloney sandwiches. They didn't have the money . . . to do the kind of studies you need."

Feeney, of course, had money, because the railroads he was working for had created a generous lobbying fund for the bill. The problem was getting the environmentalists to take it. "If you ever wanted to see a bunch of people who were skittish about dealing with railroads, it was those bearded environmentalists," Feeney said. "Hell, some of those guys had sued us a few times." The difficulty, Feeney discovered, was that the environmentalists did not want a public alliance with the railroad industry, which had a fairly egregious record of its own on ecological matters. In essence, the environmentalists told Feeney that they could not clean up the world with dirty money.

So Feeney set up a laundry.

In the lexicon of politics, a "laundry" is a device—usually a bank account established in some innocuous name—that conceals the source of money. The most notorious example was the Mexican account Richard M. Nixon's aides used in 1972 to funnel money surreptitiously from his reelection campaign to the Watergate burglars. Other, less malevolent examples pop up now and then. Whatever the morality of such deception, it is perfectly legal for a lobbyist to use a "laundry," because the statute governing lobby registrations has no strict requirements for financial accounting. Feeney's procedure for "laundering" the railroad payments to the environmentalists was fairly typical. He conjured, out of thin air, a new organization, for which he created a name (The Council for a Sound Waterways Policy), an address (a vacant office down the hall in the Western Railroads building), and a bank account. Each month he transferred some money from the railroads' lobbying fund to the Council, and the Council, in turn, transferred a monthly grant to environmental groups lobbying for waterway charges and against the Alton project. A Washington-based group, the Environmental Policy Center, which was coordinating environmental lobbying on S.790 in the capital, received $1,500 monthly under this arrangement; other organizations received aid ranging from a few books and pamphlets up to $5,000 a month while they lobbied on the railroads' behalf. For the environmental groups, this arrangement was just right. They could continue their work without ever acknowledging that they were accepting money from a major polluter. Thus when three of the groups receiving aid from Feeney testified at the Senate hearings on S.790, none mentioned any connection with the railroads. And Domenici, who was presiding at the time, didn't bother to ask, because he knew the answer would be embarrassing.

Another recipient of the railroads' largesse was the Public Interest Economics Center, a group of young, mostly liberal economists who had formed an office in Washington to provide, in their words, "some public-interest input into economic decisionmaking." Like other public-interest groups, the Center survived on grants, and before it took on any new project it first had to make sure that there was grant money available to support the effort. "We knew we wanted to work on this one," explained Lee Lane, a thoughtful young Ph.D. at the Economics Center, "because the policy of free waterways is just senseless from the economic point of view. But we needed some support. So we looked around and got a $35,000 grant from the railroads—there were no strings attached, but they knew where we stood when they gave us the money. With that, we were able to do a hell of a lot of work on the bill."

In addition to the groups whose work it paid for, the rail industry coordinated the lobbying work of various other individuals and organizations that had become interested, for one reason or another, in the waterway charge. There were public-interest groups, railroad unions, and a few groups of rail shippers. And there was a handful of odd men out—people like Charlie Schoeneman. Charles R. Schoeneman, Esq., was a classic Washington type—the well-connected tax lawyer who relied as much on know-who as on know-how to serve his clients. Among Schoeneman's clients was the Hardy Salt Company, a St. Louis firm that mined salt in Michigan and shipped it, by rail, to various Midwestern markets. In the early 1970s, Hardy ran into tough new competition for its Midwestern salt trade—and the barge industry was at the heart of the matter. One of the major barge lines landed a contract to haul sea salt produced in the Dutch Antilles up the Mississippi to the Midwest; the shipping rate was so low that the Caribbean salt sold cheaper than Hardy's Michigan product. By 1977, Hardy was seriously worried. The firm took the problem to its man in Washington, and Schoeneman realized immediately that the solution would be government action to raise the barge rates. He discussed the issue with a friend in the rail industry and was quickly invited to one of Feeney's strategy sessions on S.790. The railroads had signed up another soldier.

Despite their ingenuity at finding and funding allies, however, the railroads' lobbying operation was hindered by a serious split in the ranks over Domenici's linkage of the lock and dam with the user charge. Some members of Feeney's alliance agreed with Domenici's view that the user charge would pass only if it were attached to the Alton authorization. But Feeney refused to accept that. He and most other railroad men were strongly in favor of the user charge, all right, but they were even more strongly opposed to Lock and Dam 26. This made it difficult for the various pro-user-charge lobbyists to agree on a coordinated strategy. "This user charge is a hard enough battle anyway," Schoeneman, the salt company's lawyer, complained. "But Feeney's making it just about impossible with the strategy he's using. He wants to kill the lock and dam and then try to pass the user charge without it. If he had any brains, he'd know that one new dam is a cheap price to pay to get a nationwide system of barge tolls. But he can't see it, and that makes it tough for a guy like me to work with him."

The railroads' opponents, the barge interests, had no similar problems. Although some barge groups cared more about one issue than the other, all the forces on the barge side of the confrontation agreed that the Alton authorization should be passed and the user charge defeated. They deployed their forces to see to it that both goals were met. Over the years, the barge lines had established a network of associations and committees to lobby for the Alton project. Early in 1977, when it appeared that Domenici might get his user-charge bill to the Senate floor, a group of big barge lines and major shippers financed a new committee to concentrate on defeating the user charge. This new unit, dubbed the American Inland Waterways Committee, was set up in the office of Louis B. Susman, a tough, self-assured St. Louis lawyer who, as a member of the Democratic National Committee, had excellent political credentials. Susman also had the political sense to know that a tight lobbying battle in Congress could not be managed from St. Louis. So he went fishing for lobbyists in Washington and offered sufficiently lucrative bait to land two of the biggest.

One was a new firm called Timmons and Company, which was set up early in 1977 by William Timmons and Tom Korologos, who had been the chief lobbying agents for the Nixon and Ford Administrations. Although the two knew just about every member of Congress, their closest ties were with Republicans. For balance, therefore, Susman also retained the services of George Smathers, a smooth-talking former Senator from Florida who had good relations with Congressional Democrats. Landing Smathers was a particular coup for the barge interests. The ingratiating Floridian had left the Senate in 1968 and set up shop on K Street, N.W., the "Lobbyists' Row" of downtown Washington. One of the first clients he signed up was the Association of American Railroads, and for the next several years he had used his considerable charm and eloquence to advance railroad causes—including the waterway user charge—on Capitol Hill. Smathers was still the railroads' lobbyist when Susman approached him, early in March, with an offer from the Inland Waterways Committee. The offer was attractive enough to convince Smathers to change his spots. By April 1, George Smathers was working for the barge interests, lobbying assiduously against the user charge he had so assiduously supported while he was on the railroad payroll. As part of the arrangement, it was agreed further that Smathers' firm would take on a new partner, James Symington, a close Democratic friend of Susman's from St. Louis who had lost his seat in the House of Representatives in the 1976 election.

The sudden shift in George Smathers' allegiance attracted considerable attention in Washington's political and legal communities. It was evident now that the lobbying effort on S.790, a relatively obscure bill sponsored by an obscure first-term Senator, was going to be a big-money operation.

Smathers, after all, had been getting more than $100,000 a year from the railroads—or so the railroads said, after he left them—and it seemed clear the barge lines would have to pay at least as much to make him switch. Because the lobby registration laws do not provide for precise financial reporting, the exact amount of Smathers' fee remained an item of guesswork among Washington lawyers. Overall, however, it was just a small part of the lobbying expenditure on the user charge. By the end of the 95th Congress, the two sides would spend more than half a million dollars each, with the money pouring in from a broad range of commercial interests. Among those contributing to the railroads' lobbying cause were the makers of Dad's Root Beer and Midas Mufflers, which had corporate connections with major railroads. On the barge side, the owners of Montgomery Ward and the makers of Saran Wrap were channeling money, through their barge subsidiaries, to help defeat Domenici's bill. The strangest contribution to the lobbying treasuries came from the U.S. Steel Corporation, a multifaceted corporation so huge that it ended up lobbying on *both* sides of the user-charge issue. One U.S. Steel subsidiary, the Ohio Barge Line, Inc., contributed several thousand dollars to the fight against the user charge. At the same time, the Elgin, Joliet, and Eastern Railroad, another wholly owned U.S. Steel subsidiary, was contributing to the groups working for the charge.

While the two sides in the lobbying war were roughly equally matched financially, they adopted diametrically opposite tactics as the struggle began to heat up in the Senate. The railroads and their allies, lacking a prominent individual lobbyist who had personal connections with Senators, concentrated, on the whole, on the Senators' staffs. J. D. Feeney himself and a squadron of environmentalists tirelessly carried their message—in personal visits and voluminous literature—to every administrative assistant in the Senate. This staff strategy was a proven winner; one of the great victories in lobbying lore—the civil-rights lobby's defeat of the nomination of G. Harrold Carswell to the Supreme Court—had been won by convincing staff members, who in turn convinced their Senators, that Carswell was unfit for the Court. Since Senators were even more likely to rely on staff advice on a relatively unfamiliar issue like the waterway bill, the railroad tactic seemed eminently sensible.

But it had one hitch. While a lobbyist is making a pitch to a Senator's aide, he or she may find that the adversary has been working equally hard on the Senator. And that, in the case of S.790, was where Timmons, Korologos, Symington, and especially Smathers came in. Each of these men was on a first-name basis with members of the Senate. Placing a call to a Senator, any of the four could expect the call to be returned; meeting a Senator in the corridor or at a reception, they could count on a few minutes of face-to-face conversation—enough, usually, to lay out the grounds for voting against Domenici's bill. "It's a question of access," explained Symington. "For anyone who wants to influence the outcome of a Senate vote, access is a priceless commodity." Smathers had a special advantage in this regard. As a former Senator, he was allowed to prowl the Senate floor and the cloakrooms just off it, where Senators congregate and where most outsiders are not admitted. Smathers' sudden conversion from pro to con on the user-charge question did not seem to impair his effectiveness with his old friends in Congress. Indeed, his approaches seemed so effective that, by the first of June, Domenici began to quiver a little whenever he saw the Floridian backslapping his way through a group of former colleagues. Finally, Domenici called Brock Adams and pleaded with him to start some personal lobbying of his own. Adams did not have the same congenial relationships in the Senate that Smathers enjoyed, but his status as a cabinet member meant that Senators would pick up the telephone when Brock Adams called. By the second week in June, Adams' daily schedule included time for two or three calls to Senators every day to make a pitch for the user charge.

By that time the flow of information reaching each Senator's office about S.790 had reached the proportions of a minor flood. Domenici's allies and adversaries were sending off "Dear Colleague" letters almost every day. Brayman was not able to get the transcripts of the Senate hearings printed on an expedited basis, but he arranged to have the most favorable pieces of testimony, such as Professor Vickrey's presentation, made public anyway. To do that, he wrote a series of speeches, quoting Vickrey at length, and distributed them to Republican Senators who backed Domenici on the bill. These Senators entered the speeches, one a day, in the Congressional Record, where Brayman hoped some Senators or staff aides might take the time to read them. The barge lobby used a more complicated system. Harry Cook wrote a speech for Senator James B. Allen, an Alabama Democrat who was one of the user charge's strongest opponents, and Allen read it one day on the Senate floor. When the speech was printed the next morning in the Record, Cook reprinted the pages in a pamphlet and handed out copies to every Senator and staff aide he ran into.

Not all the lobbying was aimed directly at Capitol Hill. There was also a concerted effort, by combatants on both sides, to win the hearts and minds of the news media, on the theory that what newspapers and magazines printed about the waterway toll would influence Senators' perceptions of the issue. Late in May, a public relations firm retained by the barge industry invited about 20 reporters on a free two-day barge trip along the Ohio River. Along the way, the journalists were wined, dined, and treated to countless speeches about the need for toll-free water commerce. When the reporters got back to their desks, though, they were greeted by a thick "information packet" from the railroad industry designed to prove that the barges' "free ride" was a gross inequity.

The most important development on the media front came on the front pages of the *Washington Post*. As the biggest newspaper in Congress' hometown, the *Post* was one of the few newspapers that almost every member of Congress looked at almost every day. Accordingly, the *Post*—along with other major journals like the *New York Times* and the *Wall Street Journal*—helped determine the agenda for Washington's ongoing debate on public issues. Early in 1977, the *Post* gave the waterway user charge a prominent place on that agenda. At the start of the 95th Congress, the *Post*'s editors decided that a good way to explain the legislative process to their readers would be to pick a typical bill and follow its progress in a series of weekly articles. The editors wanted a piece of legislation that was obscure enough to be unfamiliar to most *Post* readers, but significant enough to spur a major lobbying battle. The waterway toll bill met both criteria.

When a *Post* reporter* showed up in Domenici's office in mid-February—while Rawls and Brayman were still putting the finishing touches on their draft of the legislation—the Senator could hardly believe his good fortune. As a personal matter, he was delighted with the *Post*'s idea. After four years in the U.S. Senate, Pete Domenici was still largely an unknown, even in Washington; now he was going to get some ink in the capital's most widely read newspaper. Further, Domenici thought, the *Post* could be an asset in the legislative struggle ahead—whatever the stories said about the bill. "One of the big problems with this user-charge business," the Senator explained later, "was that nobody in Congress ever thought about the inland waterways—except the guys from the big barge states. If my bill was going to get on page one of the *Post* every week, that might make people around here start thinking, 'Hey, Pete's onto a pretty good idea,' and I'd have a better chance to win."

Through the spring, as the *Post* recorded Domenici's successful effort to maneuver his bill through committee, the Senator found that his hope was borne out—particularly among his fellow Republicans.

---

* The author of this book was the *Post* reporter assigned to the story.

Most of the Republican Senators considered the *Post* a liberal, Democratic-oriented paper, and they were pleasantly surprised to see it giving regular coverage to legislation sponsored by a junior GOP Senator. In mid-June, a few days before the Senate was scheduled to vote on S.790, Senator Howard Baker, a short, cheery Republican from Tennessee who was the Senate minority leader, announced to reporters that he would vote for Domenici's user charge. This came as a surprise, because barge traffic on the Mississippi and Tennessee rivers is an important economic concern in Baker's state. "Yeah, but Pete's right on this one," Baker explained with a grin. "And anyway, I want the *Post* to show a Republican winning something for a change."

To help its members allocate their time efficiently, the Senate Democratic leadership each morning prepares a tape-recorded telephone message (224-8541) that tells the floor schedule for the day and the week ahead. Since some Republicans refuse to trust the other party on anything, the GOP has its own, separate recording (224-8601) to report the same schedule. On Friday, June 17, the two dial-a-schedule tapes mentioned the waterway user charge for the first time. Floor debate on the user charge/lock and dam bill would commence the next Wednesday, June 22, the tapes said, with a final vote likely before the end of the week. When that word went out, the members of the Senate decided that the time had come to find out what this Domenici bill was all about.

Despite the thousands of man- and woman-hours devoted to lobbying and the millions of words in pamphlets, "Dear Colleague" letters, insertions in the *Record*, and newspaper articles, most Senators who had no direct interest in the barge industry had to admit to their legislative assistants that they knew a little about the issue, but not enough to decide how to vote on it. Accordingly, Rawls and Brayman, in Domenici's office, and Tom Allison and Doug Svenson, who worked for Russell Long, the bill's leading opponent, were deluged with calls from staff aides all over the Senate. "I've got to write a floor memo for my guy so he can figure out how to vote," the staffers would say. "What's the deal on this thing, anyway?"

The news that S.790 was on the schedule also spurred a last burst of lobbying on both sides, including a final round of head counting. The head counts served only to heighten the tension, because they revealed enormous confusion in the Senate. A majority of the members were inclined to support the Lock and Dam 26 authorization, but there was no clear consensus on the user charge. Some Senators thought they would have to approve it to save the lock and dam from a veto; others were convinced that the veto threat was an empty bluff. Some Senators were convinced that the imposition of a waterway fee was a desirable policy change; others were committed to preserving the "forever free" ideal. With five days to go before S.790 reached the floor, its fate was impossible to predict.

9

Head to Head

For Pete Domenici, as for most other members of Congress, the standard items of daily apparel included a small white index card, worn in the left breast pocket, which bore, in a kind of shorthand, the Senator's schedule for the day. "7:30—bkfst., N.M. Bkrs., 316 R., PVD remarks (Lee has)," the card might begin on a typical day, meaning that Domenici's day would begin at 7:30 in room 316 of the Russell Senate Office Building in a breakfast meeting with New Mexico bankers at which Domenici was to make welcoming remarks, which Lee Rawls had written for him. Normally, the card would go on to list elements of a normal Senatorial day: a committee meeting or two, a luncheon (sometimes two), meetings with constituents, interviews with reporters, floor votes on various bills, and whatever receptions or dinners Domenici had agreed to attend after he left the Senate for the night.

On June 22, 1977, however, Domenici's white card had a single entry: "10:00—flr. debate, S.790." This was to be the most important day so far in Pete Domenici's Congressional career—the start of Senate floor action on his most important legislative initiative.

In addition to the white card, the Senator carried with him on June 22 a small green card on which Brayman had scrawled about a dozen names—the names of the Senators, according to the previous day's head count, who were still undecided on the user charge. The green

59

card was Domenici's personal lobbying assignment; to win passage of S.790, he would have to win the votes of most of the names on the list.

The green card was a concession to the fact that, despite all the high-powered lobbyists, the constituent mail, and the briefs, brochures, and broadsides that might engulf Capitol Hill over a particularly controversial issue, the most important influence on an undecided Senator is usually the personal appeal of another Senator. This parliamentary fact of life stems from the inherent clubbiness of the Senate: having been admitted to one of the world's most selective and most prestigious institutions, most members of the U.S. Senate are more likely to listen to their peers on the inside than to an outsider, no matter how imposing his or her credentials. A few days before S.790 came to the floor, accordingly, Rawls and Brayman sent Domenici forth, guided by the green card, to sell S.790 to the other members of the club.

The effectiveness of member-to-member lobbying, however, was hardly the exclusive discovery of Rawls and Brayman. In the last few days before the S.790 vote, opponents of the user charge—particularly Long, Stevenson, and John Stennis—were just as busy as the bill's backers, buttonholing their colleagues to ask for a vote against Domenici's bill. "You see," Long explained in his soft bayou drawl, "on one of these not-so-important bills—I mean, something that's not really important to anybody who doesn't have a river in his state—a lot of these Senators are not going to be thinking about this much. So if I can talk to them and get them thinking my way—just by talking personally to some Senators, that's how you win these things around here."

As the votes in the committee mark-ups had shown, the user charge was not a partisan issue; advocates and adversaries were sprinkled evenly through the two parties. Instead, the divisions on S.790 tended to be geographic, with Senators from the river states generally opposing the user charge and members from other regions more inclined to support it. Still, the personal lobbying within the Senate mostly followed party lines. Almost every Tuesday, when the Senate Republicans gathered for their weekly policy luncheon, Domenici stood up to make a pitch for his bill, reviewing the policy arguments and emphasizing that S.790 was "100 percent Republican," because there were no Democratic cosponsors. He was challenged occasionally at these sessions by John Danforth, a freshman from Missouri, who pointed out that there were no Republican co-sponsors, either. But Danforth, a pensive, introspective man who was convinced that the user charge would be disastrous for the barge industry and thus for St. Louis, his hometown, could see plainly that Domenici was making an impression on his GOP colleagues. "Every-body likes Pete anyway," Danforth said apprehensively a few days before the vote. "And a lot of guys are proud that a Republican has gotten this far with a bill of his own."

Yet, the opponents of the user charge found ways to win over some Republicans who looked, on paper, like staunch Domenici allies. The first three names on Domenici's green card list, for exam-ple—Paul Laxalt, of Nevada, and Jake Garn and Orrin G. Hatch, of Utah—were all conservative Republicans who agreed with their friend Domenici on just about everything. None of the three had any barge lines to answer to back home. But when Domenici approached Hatch one afternoon in a corner of the Senate chamber, he learned that all three votes were beyond his reach. What had happened, Domenici was told, was that Hatch had been talking to Stennis, the Mississippian who chaired the Senate subcommittee on Public Works Appropriations, about the prospects for funding for the Cen-tral Utah Project, a giant irrigation plan that was of utmost impor-tance to farmers in Utah and Nevada. Stennis laid things right on the line: if Hatch, Garn, or Laxalt were to vote for this waterway toll idea, he said, they could kiss their irrigation project goodbye for the 95th Congress. On his green card, Domenici wrote "no" next to the first three names.

Conversely, party loyalty on the Democratic side helped Domeni-ci win two others on the list, Herman E. Talmadge, of Georgia, and Jennings Randolph, of West Virginia. Randolph had voted for S.790 in the Public Works Committee, but when Domenici approached him a few days before the floor vote, the hefty West Virginian seemed noncommittal. And Talmadge, in the midst of an ugly and highly publicized divorce, was drinking heavily in the spring of 1977, mak-ing it hard for Domenici to approach him.* So Domenici referred both cases to the Administration. After some preliminary sallies from Brock Adams' lobbyists, both men received calls from Jimmy Carter himself. This was to be one of the first tests of his authority in Congress, the new President said; as Southerners and Democrats, Talmadge and Randolph owed him their support. Randolph readily agreed, after eliciting a promise that Carter would campaign person-

---

* Talmadge was eventually hospitalized for alcoholism and gave up drinking.

ally for Randolph's reelection in 1978. Talmadge, too, agreed to vote for the user charge, in the interest of Georgian solidarity—and agreed to work on his fellow Georgia Democrat, Senator Sam Nunn, as well.

It was with some trepidation that Domenici approached Barry M. Goldwater, the Arizona conservative who was one of the most senior Republicans in the Senate. Goldwater, a grumpy sort, had voted against the user charge in the Commerce Committee, and Domenici thought it might be fruitless to try to change Goldwater's mind. He tried anyway, though, and was glad he did. Goldwater explained, almost apologetically, that he had not realized what S.790 was all about when it came up, on short notice, in the Commerce mark-up. He would vote with Domenici on the floor.

On the other hand, Domenici received a disconcerting answer from Charles Percy, the Illinois Republican who had spoken so forcefully in favor of a user charge during the hearings. Percy now explained that Illinois had heavy concentrations of both barge lines and railroads, and he was being lobbied hard by both sides. With a reelection battle ahead in 1978, he was trying to figure out how he could vote on the issue without arousing the ire of either.

On the other side of the aisle, Russell Long was bringing his beguiling personality to bear on his own list of undecideds. Armed with 29 years' seniority and a major committee chairmanship, Long was a formidable foot soldier in any legislative battle. When Talmadge told Long about his commitment to the President, Long refused to give up. He kept talking about his long friendship with Talmadge, and their common interest in various bills pending before Long's Finance Committee. Eventually Long received an "if you need me" pledge from the Georgian—if the Senate roll call on the user charge came down to one vote, Talmadge would switch and join Long in opposition. When Long talked to William V. Roth, Jr., a Delaware Republican, a state that had a significant railroad presence, the chairman knew just what to say. Roth promised to vote against the user charge in return for Long's promise that Finance would report favorably on Roth's pet tax bill, an income tax credit for parents paying college tuition.

The most striking demonstration of Long's authority in the Senate was the case of Daniel Patrick Moynihan, a first-year Democrat from New York. Early in April, a railroad lobbyist had asked Moynihan about S.790. The Senator, sounding like the professor he once had been, reeled off a long exegesis about the Erie Canal and New York

State's barge boom in the early nineteenth century. In the twentieth century, though, Moynihan went on, the canals were dry, and it wouldn't make much sense for a New Yorker to vote to continue a subsidy to the barge industry. Moynihan, the lobbyist decided, was a safe vote. But by mid-June, when the railroad man made a routine return visit to Moynihan's office, the professor had forgotten his own lesson. In the interim, Moynihan had been appointed to the Finance Committee, and Long had made it clear that the user-charge vote would be a test of loyalty for all committee Democrats. "I think I'll probably go along with the chairman," Moynihan said, and the lobbyist retreated in dismay.

Still, Long and his allies on the anti-user-charge front faced some serious problems. There was, after all, a veto threat. The barge lines' lobbying position was that this threat was a bluff—that Jimmy Carter would not dare veto a bill as popular as the Lock and Dam 26 authorization, even if there were no user charge attached. Some Senators accepted this reasoning, but many did not. Further, the opponents of the user charge had difficulty coming up with policy arguments to support continuation of toll-free transit on waterways. It was difficult to talk around the fact that the taxpayers were providing a costly service, free of charge, to a profitable private industry. To avoid that difficulty, Long and his supporters agreed that their opposition to S.790 would be based on the argument that the user charge had not been adequately studied—that more analysis was needed before Congress could implement such an important policy change. But that argument, too, had a built-in problem: more than a dozen public and private groups had studied the question, and almost all had concluded that imposition of a waterway toll was long overdue.

Six days before S.790 was due to come to the floor, the barge lobby's chief head counters, Tom Korologos and Harry Cook, reported to Long that the vote was going to be perilously close. The safest thing to do, they said, would be to filibuster. If Long and his colleagues could keep the debate going long enough, delaying a vote, the Senate leadership might decide to take S.790 off the schedule for a few weeks. That would give the barge lines a better chance to win the battle. Long, whose own political antennae had sensed a tight struggle ahead, agreed that this made sense. But when he broached the idea to his Senate allies, they responded angrily. Putting off the user charge, they said, would postpone a final decision on Lock and Dam 26 as well.

The angriest objection to the filibuster idea came from Danforth, the 40-year-old Republican from Missouri. A tall, handsome heir to the Ralston Purina fortune, Danforth had spent two years at Yale Divinity School between college and law school, and he brought with him to the Senate a moralist's sense of right and wrong. Danforth said it would be simply unfair to deprive Domenici of an up-or-down vote after he had worked so hard to get his bill to the floor. To Long, who thought it was a Senator's job to use the rules when he could to pass bills he favored and to defeat those he opposed, the notion of "fairness" seemed beside the point. But he agreed to think some more about the filibuster plan. By the morning of June 22, when S.790 was called up for consideration, Long had still not decided what to do.

The final days before the vote also provoked feverish lobbying from all the interest groups working on the bill—the railroads, the environmentalists, and the Administration on Domenici's side, and the barge industry, the water-freight shippers, and various unions lined up with Long. Long met almost daily with the barge lobbyists to thrash out the pros and cons of the filibuster idea and to coordinate lobbying. Rawls and Brayman had a planning session every morning with people from the Administration and the railroads to map the day's effort: "Who's going to talk to Kennedy? Who's got a contact on Percy's staff?" Domenici received help, too, from some of his Senate colleagues who had an interest in the user-charge idea. One of his most useful allies in the Senate was Gaylord A. Nelson, a liberal Democrat from Wisconsin who had been trying for years to find a way to curb the power of the Corps of Engineers. The user charge seemed a possible means to that end, and so Nelson, an effervescent type who had good friends in the Senate's liberal bloc (where Domenici's ties were weak), lobbied hard to win Democratic votes—from liberals like Edmund S. Muskie, of Maine; Joseph R. Biden, Jr., of Delaware; and Donald W. Riegle, Jr., of Michigan—for the New Mexico Republican's bill.

The U.S. Senate chamber is a three-story-high rectangle about as big as the varsity gym at a medium-sized Midwestern college. At the front of the room is a long marble table where the presiding officer sits, surrounded by various clerks and vote counters, and arching outward in a semicircle from that table are 100 small brown desks. Traditionally, the Democrats sit at the desks on the left side of the semicircle and the Republicans on the right. Although the Democrats have held a majority in the Senate for the last two decades, artful furniture arrangement makes it appear that the room is equally divided between the two parties, with a broad center aisle separating the Republicans' desks from the Democrats'. The front-row desks on either side of this aisle are normally reserved for the two party leaders, but when a bill is up for debate, the leadership seats are taken by the chairpersons and ranking minority member of the committee or subcommittee that has jurisdiction over the legislation.

When the debate on S.790 opened at 10 o'clock on June 22, Domenici, flanked by Rawls and Brayman, was in the front-row aisle seat on the Republican side, and Gravel, with two staff aides, was across from him. The only other members present were Danforth, far back on the right; Long, midway behind Gravel; and Stevenson, just behind Long. Since the first two were committed in favor of the user charge and the latter three were committed against it, a newcomer to the Senate might well have wondered why anybody bothered to debate. "Yeah, that's a question everybody asks," Brayman explained. "For one thing, a lot of members come over to the floor for one thing or another during the day, and they'll, you know, usually stand around and listen for a few minutes. And then most offices send at least one staff guy to sit in the gallery and take notes, so you're debating for the staff and you hope they'll pass the good stuff on to their Senator. And then I think it's just that Senators don't like to vote on anything unless they've talked about it for a while, even if nobody's listening."

Near the beginning of the floor debate, the backers of the user charge suffered a mild parliamentary setback. Soon after Domenici formally called up his legislation—containing the Lock and Dam 26 authorization and the user-charge provision—Stevenson sent to the desk an amendment to Domenici's bill that retained the authorization but struck the user-charge provision, calling instead for an 18-month study of the user-charge question, with no Congressional action until the study was completed. Under the Senate rules, Stevenson's amendment would be the first item to come up for a vote. This confused matters somewhat—as Stevenson knew it would —because it meant that Domenici's supporters would have to cast a "nay" vote to vote in favor of the user charge. If one or two members failed to grasp that subtlety, Domenici might lose the whole fight. On the other hand, Stevenson stood to lose if the confusion struck his own supporters.

For the first five hours, the debate was alternately comatose and crackling. There were long, dull speeches punctuated every now and then by angry, shouted exchanges between proponents and opponents of the waterway toll. Although there were a few Senators who opposed the rebuilding of Lock and Dam 26 (Gary Hart, the Colorado Democrat, called the project "the B-1 bomber of our national transportation policy"), most raised no question about that part of the bill. The only seriously contested issue was whether a user charge would be linked to the authorization. Domenici kept trying to argue for the linkage on policy grounds, and Long, Stevenson, and Danforth kept raising policy objections. Gravel, true to form, skipped the policy points and cut to the heart of the matter: "These two issues are married together for a very good reason," he rasped in one particularly heated exchange with Stevenson, "and the good reason is we don't have a prayer of getting through user charges in the House if we do not have Lock and Dam 26 tied to it."

At 3:15 Russell Long, who had left to attend a committee meeting, came back into the chamber carrying the text of an enormous speech and two huge statute books with scores of pages marked for reference. He snapped his fingers at a page and asked for a lectern and a pitcher of drinking water. Evidently the Senator from Louisiana was settling in for a long stay.

At just about this time, however, Harry Cook, who was marshaling the barge lobbying team from a spot in the lobby just off the Senate floor, came on two important pieces of intelligence. Senator Lloyd M. Bentsen, a Texas Democrat whom the head counters considered a user-charge supporter, had been called home for a funeral. Senator Edmund Muskie, a Maine Democrat who was openly committed to vote with Domenici, had flown to New York to make a speech. With those two men absent, according to Cook's latest tabulation, the opponents would have a majority. If the vote were put off a day or two, both would probably be back in Washington. Cook sent an urgent message in to Danforth, who stepped quickly across the floor and started a whispered conversation with Long and Stevenson. In a few seconds, the men were nodding in agreement, and Long turned to address the Senate.

"I was discussing with the Senators the parliamentary situation," Long began in his folksy, casual manner. "While I would like to make my speech in extenso, I believe most people have heard my views on this matter already. . . . I would suggest . . . that we limit debate to half an hour, and at the end of the half-hour, we vote."

At the front of the room, Rawls, Brayman, Domenici, and Gravel huddled to consider this surprising development. All four knew, of course, that Long must have decided he had the votes to win. But

Domenici, who had been receiving new head counts all day from Sue Williams, Brock Adams' ace head counter, thought he had the votes. There was no need to drag things out any longer.

At 3:58 a single long buzzer sounded on the Senate side of the Capitol and through the hallways and offices of the Senate office buildings at the northern edge of the Capitol grounds—the signal for a roll-call vote. From the galleries, a swarm of staffers came down to meet their Senators at the door and explain that a "nay" vote on Stevenson's amendment was a vote for the user charge. The elevators just outside the floor flashed the message "Members Only," so that Senators coming into the Capitol would not be delayed on their way to cast their votes.

In a deep voice and a slow, deliberate cadence, the tally clerk began to call the roll of the Senate. At the moment he came to "Missss ... ter ... Do ... men ... i ... ci," the vote was tied, so Domenici's "nay" put his side ahead for a moment or two. Soon thereafter, Goldwater came hobbling down the aisle on his cane, followed by Baker: two more nays. Talmadge, without a glance at Long or Domenici, voted "nay," and when Nunn, the junior Senator from Georgia, came in and cast a "nay" vote as well, Brayman broke into a smile. Obviously, the Administration had been working on the Democrats. Brayman's smile grew noticeably broader when Henry Bellmon, a Republican from Oklahoma, came down the aisle and uttered a quiet "nay"; Bellmon was Domenici's closest friend in the Senate, but he also had the Arkansas River waterway at home, and his voice had been in doubt. Moynihan came through the door next and strode up to glance at the tally sheet. While he was there, Long came over for a brief conversation, and then Moynihan raised his hand to get the clerk's attention. "Aye," he said crisply. Roth added his "aye" a few minutes later, but by then it was too late.

All this time a distinguished, silver-haired man had been standing by himself at the front of the chamber with a look of anguish on his face. This was Percy, who was following the roll call vote by vote, checking the tally clerk's ballot sheet now and then to check the totals. When the presiding officer began to announce that "all time has expired," the vote stood at 51 "nays" to 43 "ayes"—and then Percy finally voted: "Aye." With that, he might be able to mollify both sides. He would tell the barge interests in his state that he supported them by voting for Stevenson's study amendment, and he could tell the railroads back home that he had waited until he was sure they would win before he voted against them.

"On this vote," the clerk intoned in the same careful cadence, "the ayes are 44, the nays are 51, and the amendment offered by the gentleman from Illinois is rejected."

On the floor, Domenici, beaming like a schoolboy who had just batted in the winning run, accepted a congratulatory handshake from Gravel. Rawls and Brayman looked at each other and shook their heads in happy disbelief—they had never, never expected a margin as big as seven votes. Danforth went over to shake Domenici's hand, and then walked back and slumped dejectedly into his chair. Stevenson stood deadly still, looking ill. Long, sucking on a long cigar, looked over his list of undecideds to see who had deserted him. In the press gallery, the reporters clattered up the steps to call in the news to their editors. "You'll never guess what happened," Ann Cooper, of *Congressional Quarterly* magazine, shouted into a telephone. "Pete Domenici went head to head with Russell Long—and Domenici won!"

10

The Blue Slip

With the defeat of Stevenson's effort to kill the user charge, Senate passage of the Domenici bill became a foregone conclusion. Senators who were anxious to pass the Lock and Dam 26 authorization had no option other than Domenici's combined lock and dam/user-charge legislation, and when S.790 finally came up for a vote, just before 7:00 PM, it passed by a margin of 71 to 20. Immediately afterward, Gravel stood up and proposed that the language of the bill just passed be inserted into a House bill, H.R.5885. This was the omnibus rivers and harbors bill the House had passed a few weeks before, and Gravel's move was part of the strategy Domenici had devised to get the user charge through the House. By making their bill part of a bill already passed by the House, the Senators could send the user-charge provision directly to a conference committee. If the House conferees would accept it, the user charge would be likely to pass on the House floor.

Inserting Senate-passed language into a House-passed bill is a fairly standard parliamentary device, so Gravel's proposal was approved without objection. It looked as if the waterway bill would sail smoothly along on its charted course. In fact, though, the legislation was sailing right into a Constitutional trap.

For anyone who had listened carefully during the Senate's consideration of the user charge, the trap should not have been a com-

69

plete surprise. In the hearings before the Water Resources Subcommittee, a lawyer representing the barge interests had argued that
Domenici's bill violated a clause in the Constitution that prohibits
the Senate from originating revenue-raising legislation. Stevenson
had brought up the same objection during the floor debate. Although
Rawls had prepared a long legal memorandum to rebut the Constitutional argument, Domenici did not even bother to answer it on the
floor. "I just figured Adlai was throwing in every argument he could
come up with," the Senator explained later. "You had to go back
pretty far in history to find a place where that origination clause had
really been enforced."

Historically, at least, Domenici was right. The clause in question
—Article I, Section 7, of the Constitution, which states that "All Bills
for raising Revenue shall originate in the House of Representatives"
—was based on eighteenth-century practice in the British Parlia-
ment, where only the House of Commons, which was considered the
more representative of the two houses, could originate tax levies. In
the early Congresses, as the two houses were sorting out their respec-
tive powers, the origination clause had been the focus of numerous
arguments. In the last quarter of the nineteenth century, when Congress was enacting a broad range of new federal taxes, the clause
became a favorite tool of lawyers who wanted to challenge the legal-
ity of a particular tax; if you looked hard enough, you could find
some Senate input into almost any tax bill, and this was the basis
of various suits arguing that new taxes were unconstitutional. The
courts, for the most part, were wary of stepping into disputes pitting
one house of Congress against another, and so federal judges developed a test that permitted them to sidestep the issue almost every
time. If the legislation was mainly "regulatory," and the revenue-
raising aspect was merely "incidental," the courts said, the origination clause would not void a bill that started in the Senate. Under
this rationale, the Supreme Court in 1897 upheld a Senate-originated
tax on bank notes, stating that the main purpose of the legislation
was to regulate banking. A Senate bill raising property taxes in the
District of Columbia was upheld in 1906 on the grounds that it was
actually a transportation law, since proceeds from the tax increase
were to be used to build a new rail depot in the capital. (The depot,
Union Station, was built, and still stands today.)

The water-freight lobbyists, however, were not challenging S.790
in a court of law. They took their case to a much more receptive
forum—the House of Representatives. Whatever its status in the law-
books, the origination clause was dear to the hearts of the members of

the House. They were jealous of their prerogatives, and they reacted resentfully whenever it appeared that the Senate was treading on their Constitutionally protected turf. Accordingly, when a delegation of barge lobbyists raised the origination clause issue with Representative Al Ullman, an Oregon Democrat who chaired the House Ways and Means Committee, a few days after S.790 had been passed in the Senate, Ullman was immediately sympathetic. This was partly because, as the House's chief tax expert, Ullman was particularly on guard against Senate incursions into his jurisdiction, and partly because most of the timber and farm products produced in his rugged northeast Oregon district moved to market by barge down the Columbia River. Ullman's first response was to ask Ways and Means' staff director, John Martin, to look into the origination clause question. Martin was quickly engulfed in lengthy legal briefs from both sides arguing whether Domenici's bill was more "revenue raising" than "regulatory," but before he was able to plow through them, Ullman went ahead with the next step. He formally asked that H.R.5885 be held at the Speaker's desk, without being sent to conference. And he asked the Clerk of the House to dig out a copy of the standard form letter—an ornate document printed on a blue slip of paper—by which the House informs "the other body" that the origination clause has been violated. Al Ullman was going to defend the honor of the House—but he was going to defeat the user charge in the process.

Under House rules, a majority vote on the House floor would be necessary to authorize dispatch of the blue slip. But this was a formality; House members were unlikely to vote against Ullman if he decided that their prerogatives had been impinged on. And if a blue slip were issued, the Senate-passed waterway bill would become a legal nullity—and the Senate would have no recourse.

From his perch on the Senate side of the Capitol, Russell Long watched these rapid developments with undisguised delight. Although the homespun gentleman from Louisiana was not usually given to literary references, he could not resist observing that the whole scenario reminded him of Robert Louis Stevenson's *Treasure Island*. In that tale, which Long had read as a boy, the pirates exchanged death threats by passing notes marked with "the Black Spot." Now the House was conveying the same message via "the Blue Slip."

Pete Domenici, of course, was hardly delighted. Less than two weeks after its triumph on the Senate floor, Domenici's pet bill was in dire trouble.

11

The Speaker Speaks

One of the most common progressions in American political life is the leap from the House of Representatives to a seat in the Senate. To most House members, "the other body," with its smaller membership, greater prestige, and—especially—six-year term begins to look extremely attractive after three or four terms in the confused hurly-burly of the House. At any given time, about one-third of the members of the Senate are veterans of service in the House; and it is probably safe to say that, at any given time, about two-thirds of the members of the House are thinking about running for the Senate someday. Like every political rule, though, this axiom has its famous exceptions. One Congressman who never aspired to move up was Gerald Ford. When Michigan Republican leaders offered then Congressman Ford the party's Senate nomination in 1964, Ford replied, as one GOP leader recalls it, "No thanks—if I just stay in the House long enough, I might be Speaker someday."

Another Congressman who held the same ambition—and saw it realized—was Thomas P. (Tip) O'Neill, Jr., the savvy Boston Irishman who was elected Speaker of the House by his fellow Democrats at the beginning of the 95th Congress. O'Neill, who was 64 years old when he reached that long-desired goal, had come to Congress in 1952, taking over a seat that was vacated by another Irishman, John F. Kennedy (who left the House to run for the Senate). The moment he first stepped inside the House chamber in Washington, O'Neill knew that he would love the place. One reason might have been that O'Neill, an imposing, white-haired figure with a booming voice, was too colorful to get lost, even in the midst of 434 other politicians who were constantly striving for attention. But O'Neill's emotional attachment to the House stemmed as well from his conviction that it was the real seat of American democracy. One of the tasks assigned to O'Neill, as he moved his way up the leadership ladder in the House, was to greet each new crop of freshly elected Democrats at the start of each new Congress. In that biennial session, O'Neill would remind the new members that, when a Senator died or retired during his or her term, the seat was usually filled by a gubernatorial appointment until the next election. But when a House seat became vacant a special election was always called to fill it. "Only the voters, only the people, can put you in the House of Representatives," O'Neill would roar. "And you know why? You know why? BECAUSE THIS IS THE PEOPLE'S HOUSE!"

O'Neill's other great passion in life was the Democratic Party. He was a party man through and through, and there was no one in America happier than Tip O'Neill when the Democrats regained the White House in the 1976 election. In January 1977, when Jimmy Carter took over as President and Tip O'Neill took over as Speaker, O'Neill was determined to show the nation what a Democratic President and a Democratic Congress could achieve together.

Thus when the prospect of a blue slip threatened to sink the waterway user charge legislation, O'Neill was caught in an uncomfortable tug-of-war between his two loyalties.

It was Brock Adams who put the problem in O'Neill's lap. Adams had been out of town when the blue-slip controversy arose, and when he came back to Washington he was astonished to learn that the waterway bill was suddenly in serious danger. Domenici, of course, was powerless in this situation, and Adams knew better than to drag the President into a dispute between the two houses of Congress. So he took the problem to O'Neill. O'Neill and Adams had become good friends during their years in Congress, and O'Neill had been one of the chief proponents of Brock Adams for a cabinet office when Carter was forming his Administration.

The Speaker, accordingly, felt a patron's obligation to help when Adams called about the blue-slip problem. Moreover, O'Neill personally felt that a waterway user charge was an eminently reasonable reform. He knew, too, that the Lock and Dam 26 authorization was almost sure to pass in the 95th Congress, and he had no desire to get the House involved in a veto and a drawn-out effort to override the veto. From the point of view of the House's agenda, the best thing to do would be to pass some kind of combination legislation containing the Alton authorization and a user charge—something like S.790 —and get the issue out of the way as quickly as possible.

On the other hand, O'Neill felt that he could not let S.790 go unchallenged. Like Winston Churchill, who declared that he had "not become the King's First Minister to preside over the liquidation of the British Empire," O'Neill wanted everyone to know that he had not become Speaker to stand by quietly while the Senate violated the House's Constitutional prerogatives. Caught between his loyalty to the Democratic Administration and his loyalty to the House, O'Neill saw a clear need for a compromise. And Tip O'Neill was a compromiser par excellence. He began talking to the interested parties—to Adams, to Ullman, to Ray Roberts, a Texan who chaired the House Public Works Subcommittee that had jurisdiction over the Lock and Dam 26 authorization, and to Harold T. (Bizz) Johnson, the California Congressman who chaired the full Public Works Committee. Adams, of course, insisted that a user-charge provision had to be part of any bill authorizing the Alton project. Ullman, Roberts, and Johnson were unhappy with that proposition, but O'Neill convinced them that the veto threat made it a necessity. Ullman was adamant, however, that the Ways and Means Committee should have jurisdiction over the user-charge portion of the bill; he would not stand for a procedure like the Senate's, where the tax-writing committee had been left out of the picture. Moreover, the three chairmen, prodded by barge lobbyists, maintained that the Senate-passed user-charge formula would be much too costly for the barges. O'Neill took all this in and then, in a "summit meeting" with the principals in his office in mid-July, the Speaker spoke.

To avoid the origination problem, O'Neill said, H.R.5885 would be left to die and the House would originate its own version of S.790. Johnson's committee would approve a new lock and dam authorization. Ullman's committee would write a waterway tax bill, setting the charge considerably lower than the Senate version. The two measures would be linked on the House floor, passed, and sent to the Senate as a new bill. It had taken the Senate five months to achieve that much, but O'Neill said he couldn't wait that long. There were major House debates coming up on the farm bill and Carter's energy legislation. To clear the way, this relatively minor issue was to be reported out of both committees within two weeks. O'Neill would then get it to the floor as quickly as possible.

Like most compromises, O'Neill's plan left everybody unhappy in one way or another. Adams was worried that, when the House's tax bill was sent to the Senate, it would be assigned to the Finance Committee, where Long would have a new chance to upset the whole arrangement. The barge lobbyists were again being told that they would have to accept a waterway charge to get the Alton authorization. The railroads were angry that O'Neill was willing to accept a lower waterway fee than the Senate version. But all sides realized that there was not much choice; O'Neill's plan seemed to be the only way out of the bind. The compromise was given the grudging consent of all concerned. The waterway bill was back on course.

12

"The Fix Is In"

When the Water Resources Subcommittee of the House Public Works Committee opened its hearings on the waterway-toll bill at 10:00 on July 18—exactly five days and 21 hours after the summit meeting in Tip O'Neill's office—the standing-room-only audience was treated to an historic first: a representative of the barge industry expressed support for a waterway user charge. The spokesman, Ramsay Potts, a prosperous-looking Washington lawyer who had been a lobbyist for the barge interests for years, did not hide his distaste for the idea, but he conceded to the committee that the barge lines were at the point of surrender. "We recognize," Potts said unhappily, "that if we're going to get legislation to replace Lock and Dam 26, we have to—that is, we may have to—accept some form of user tax."

That concession had been agreed to in an emotional meeting of barge-line executives and their Washington lobbyists two days after O'Neill had laid down the law. "It took a lot of soul-searching," J. W. Hershey, president of one of the nation's largest barge lines, recalled later. "After having worked 35 years to defend the waterways from any form of user charges, here I was agreeing to it." The barge lines, except for a minority faction that refused to budge, had concluded that they would have to pay a price—a user charge—to win House passage of the Alton authorization. They left open the possibility of working to strike the user-charge provision when the bill went back to the Senate, but for the present, at least, they agreed to accept the unacceptable.

Having gone that far, however, they were determined to make the user charge as painless as possible. They decided that the charge should take the form of a diesel-fuel tax, rather than the tolls and license fees contemplated in S.790. A fuel tax, unlike a toll or a fee, would be the province of Long's Finance Committee in the Senate and Ullman's Ways and Means Committee in the House. If there had to be some waterway charge, the barge lines felt, it would be nice to keep it under the thumbs of those friendly chairmen. Finally, the barge lines had to decide a question central to every tax bill: how much? They originally suggested a tax of 1 cent per gallon, but when they brought up that figure in private meetings with Ullman and with Johnson, the Public Works chairman, both members said it was ridiculously low. The smallest tax Ullman thought he could propose without jeopardizing the lock and dam bill was 4 cents per gallon —the same as the federal fuel tax car and truck drivers pay. The barge lines decided to go along.

By the time the House hearings opened, then, all the important issues had been privately resolved. For this reason, and because of the truncated schedule O'Neill had dictated, the Water Resources Subcommittee held only one day of hearings. The witnesses' major area of disagreement was the rate of fuel tax to be imposed. Dempsey, of the railroad association, argued that the barges should pay enough for the government to recover every cent of the $500 million or so it spent each year to build new waterways and maintain old ones. To do that, Dempsey said, the fuel tax should be set at 64 cents per gallon. Brock Adams said the tax should take in as much money as the tolls and fees established by S.790 would have. The Senate bill was designed to recover all of the government's annual maintenance costs, and half of the money spent on new construction, for a total of about $350 million per year. To do that, Adams said, the tax should be set at 42 cents per gallon. And then Potts, speaking for the barge industry, made his presentation: "Mr. Chairman, we do not favor any tax at all, but if there is to be a tax, we urge that it not be greater than 4 cents a gallon."

If Potts was unhappy about the message he was forced to bear, he was followed to the witness table by an individual who was downright angry about the state of affairs—Berkley Bedell. After all, Bedell was the sponsor of the first user-charge bill introduced in the House in the 95th Congress, and he was the only person on the House side who had done anything about it until the Senate forced the issue. But then Bedell had been left out in the cold. He heard about O'Neill's summit meeting only after it was over; and then, when he came to testify at the subcommittee hearing, he could sense that a private deal had been struck. "Oh, I was pretty pissed off when I saw what had happened," the normally mild-mannered Iowan recalled later. "I mean, by the time I knew what was up, the whole thing was kind of a fait accompli." Bedell, who had no particular urge to be at the center of things, was upset not because he had been left out of the decisionmaking process, but because of the decision that had been made—the decision to impose a flat-rate fuel tax on waterway traffic. As far as Bedell was concerned, that approach was dead wrong. It ignored a principle that had prompted him to introduce a user-charge bill in the first place: the principle of capital recovery.

"Capital recovery" is economists' language for the idea that any fee for use of government-built facilities should include a direct linkage between the government's expenditures on the facility and the amount of the fee. As applied to waterways, this meant a fee structured so that whenever the government's spending on waterways went up, the fees paid by waterway users would increase, too. This principle was reflected in the Senate bill, S.790, and was, in fact, one of Pete Domenici's basic arguments for S.790—that if each new improvement on the waterways added to the barge lines' costs, the political pressure for expensive new improvements would be sharply decreased. As Bedell explained it to the subcommittee, "The users are going to be anxious not to see facilities built that need not be built or not overbuilt, because they will be paying part of the cost of those facilities." Although Domenici had made various changes in S.790 as it moved toward passage, the Senate bill had always retained the linkage between the costs paid by the government and the charges imposed on the users. The Senate bill, for this reason, did not say how much the barges should pay in any given year. It directed the executive branch to publish a new schedule of charges each year, based on the government's expected level of spending that year.

The proposal for a flat-rate fuel tax, however, negated that principle. Under a flat-rate system, the barge lines would be paying the same tax no matter how many hundreds of millions of dollars the Corps of Engineers spent on the waterways. The barge lines would have no reason to stop pressing Congress for new and bigger water projects. "Whenever the users are not paying any of the costs," Bedell complained in his testimony, "then there is no one there to look after the taxpayers' money."

Bedell's closest ally on the Public Works Committee was Robert W. Edgar, a Democrat from Pennsylvania who had entered Congress the same year Bedell did and became a close friend. Edgar, too, believed in a user charge that incorporated the cost-recovery principle, but he told Bedell to save his breath. "The fix is in," Edgar said.

That became evident over the next few days. The morning after its one-day hearing, the Water Resources Subcommittee held a mark-up and reported out a waterway bill along the lines that had been agreed to in the bargemen's private meetings with Ullman and Johnson. The next day, the full Public Works Committee held its mark-up, and approved the subcommittee's bill. The day after the Public Works mark-up, Ways and Means began its hearings on the fuel-tax plan, with all the same witnesses who had testified three days earlier presenting the same testimony over again. This time, Adams proposed a tax of 40 cents per gallon—2 cents lower than the figure he had suggested in the earlier hearing—but Ullman wouldn't hear of it. "Totally out of the ballpark," the chairman said.

The Ways and Means hearings ended on a Friday, and the following Monday morning the committee met to mark up the bill. The weekend break had given the railroad lobbyists a chance to voice their bitter complaints about the deal that let the barge lines get away with nothing more than a 4-cent tax, however, so when the committee met there was general agreement that the fuel tax would have to be somewhat higher. But not much. After rejecting a string of proposals for a tax of 12, 10, and 8 cents a gallon, the committee finally agreed to set the tax at 4 cents for the first two years and 6 cents thereafter. A few members complained about the haste that had marked the bill's consideration—"How can I vote on a tax bill when the language isn't even written yet?" asked Abner J. Mikva, an Illinois Democrat—but Ullman had no intention of slowing down. When the bill came up for final committee approval, Ullman called for a voice vote and announced the results all in one breath. "All in favor say 'aye,' all opposed 'nay,' " he rattled off, not pausing at all to let the members vote. "Theayeshaveitandthemotionisagreedto." The chairman then directed the committee staff to work with Public Works

staff and prepare a joint committee report—in one day. Two weeks
after they started the process, the two committees had reported out a
waterway bill—right on Tip O'Neill's schedule.

It was obvious now that the bill was sliding down a greased chute
toward easy passage on the House floor—but then O'Neill himself
plucked it off. Among the several bills lined up behind the waterway
measure on the calendar was a major reenactment of federal farm
legislation. Congressmen from rural districts were anxious to finish
work on the farm bill before they went home for the August recess;
they appealed to O'Neill to move it forward on the schedule. Since
accommodating that kind of request is an important means for a
Speaker to build up goodwill, O'Neill wanted to be accommodating.
Moving the farm bill forward would mean that the waterway legislation would have to be put off until after the recess. But it would also
mean that Tip O'Neill would have dozens of farm-state Congressmen
in his debt. The waterway bill was put off.

When the members of the House returned to Washington after
Labor Day, the waterway bill, having been reported favorably by two
committees and blessed by the leadership, was one of the first candidates for action on the floor. Before it could get there, though, the bill
had to stop off in one more committee. To gain admission to the
floor, a House bill needs a ticket—in parliamentary jargon, a "rule."
The ticket booth is the Rules Committee. It controls the flow of
legislation to the floor by parceling out tickets, or rules, that establish
when a bill can come up, how much debate there will be, what kinds
of points of order will be allowed, and what kinds of amendments
can be offered. (In the Senate, these details of floor consideration are
usually worked out by verbal agreements made right on the floor. But
with 435 members, the House is too unruly for that.)

Like most traditional institutions, the Rules Committee has developed parlance and procedures all its own. There are "open rules"
—permitting almost any amendment when a bill comes up on the
floor—and "closed rules"—permitting no amendments—and various shades of rule in between. When Ullman came before the Rules
Committee in September to get a rule for the waterway bill, he asked
for a "modified open rule"—permitting certain types of amendments
and prohibiting others. Specifically, the rule he asked for would
have permitted floor amendments to reduce the fuel tax approved by
the committees, but would have prohibited any amendment to increase it. Such a rule seemed just right to Ullman, who wanted the

To the unenthusiastic applause of its erstwhile opponents, the waterway user charge became the law of the land. Among those present, from left to right: Susan Williams, Department of Transportation; Brock Adams; James Oberstar, D. Rep. —Minn.; Muriel Humphrey, D. Sen.— Minn.; Wendell Anderson, D. Sen.—Minn. (blonde behind President Carter); Bruce Vento, D. Rep. —Minn.; Rick Nolan, D. Rep. —Minn. (Photo by Bill Fitz-Patrick, The White House.)

A weary Pete Domenici was campaigning in a uranium mine in Grants, New Mexico, when Lee Rawls called: "We're getting screwed." (U.S. Senate photo.)

Russell Long was just a "good old boy" from Baton Rouge who became a master of politics and procedure in the U.S. Senate. (Photo by James K. W. Atherton, *The Washington Post*.)

From the pilothouse of Bernard G., John McNeil looked out over a nest of barges that covered five acres of river. (Photo by Ken Feil, The Washington Post.)

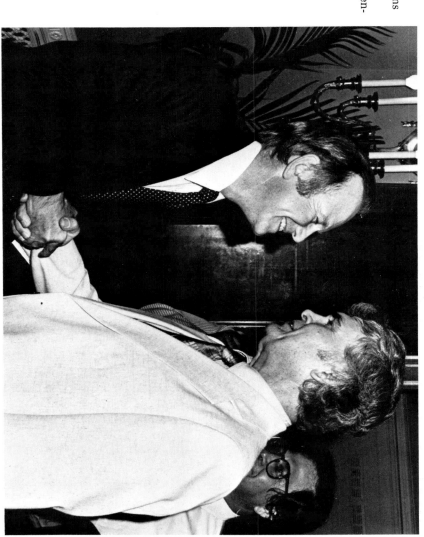

When "the blue slip" threatened to sink the waterway bill, Brock Adams (left) paid a friendly call on Al Ullman to find out what was happening. (Photo by Joe Heiberger, The Washington Post.)

Berkley Bedell first heard about the waterway user charge idea in meetings with his constituents, like this one in a church basement in Lake City, Iowa. (U.S. House of Representatives photo.)

When Russell Long (left) started lobbying Patrick Moynihan, Professor Moynihan forgot his own history lesson. (Wide World Photos.)

Lee Rawls (left) and Hal Brayman knew that Senator Pete Domenici (center) would be just about the perfect sponsor for Brayman's pet bill. (U.S. Senate photo.)

waterway fee kept as small as possible. But some members of the Rules Committee were dubious. Wouldn't it be fairer, they asked, if the rule permitted amendments to increase the tax as well as to cut it? This line of questioning was cut off by the gruff, stentorian voice of the Rules Committee chairman, Democrat James J. Delaney, of New York, a 76-year-old Congressional fixture who thought it impudent for junior members to disagree with a committee chairman. "If we open this thing up," Delaney snorted, "we'll never get a bill off the floor."

Ullman was followed to the witness table by Bedell and Edgar, who asked for a rule permitting one specific amendment—an amendment to increase the tax. Bedell, who was still angry about the absence of a capital-recovery provision, made an impassioned plea, and when he finished, the Rules Committee seemed uncertain how to proceed. Eventually, the members settled on a compromise between the Ullman and Bedell positions: the fuel tax would go to the floor under a closed rule, permitting only one vote, yes or no, on the 4- to 6-cent fuel tax.

With the rule taken care of, the waterway bill needed only to be placed on the House calendar for debate and a vote on the floor. But that was not as simple as it seemed. There was a considerable post-recess backlog of bills due for final floor action, and the waterway measure had to be sandwiched in among them. The sandwich-maker was Gary Hymel, O'Neill's chief staff aide, whose responsibilities included putting together the House's weekly schedule of floor activity. The scheduling process was Hymel's least favorite job, because it was a constant point of friction between the Speaker's office and the members of the House. The Speaker had an interest in keeping the schedule fluid, so that exigencies like the farm-bill vote could be accommodated. But the members liked the schedules to be firmly established well in advance, so that lobbyists could be alerted and "Dear Colleague" letters could be dispatched at the proper moment before a particular bill came to the floor. The waterway bill posed particular problems. Bedell had promised to wage a floor fight against the closed rule, in addition to the debate on the bill itself, but Hymel could not find a bloc of time big enough to handle both the rule fight and the bill itself. Eventually, he came up with a plan to squeeze the measure onto the floor in three segments.

A debate and vote on the rule would be scheduled for Thursday, October 6. Debate on the bill itself would start the following Tuesday, but there was not enough time available to finish it that day. It seemed logical, then, to continue the debate the next day, but O'Neill had targeted that day for the House to act on one of his pet projects. The waterway bill would be put off again—with the final debate and vote on Thursday, October 13. This meant, of course, that it would be almost impossible for members to get a coherent idea of the issues involved from the floor debate—but that was not uncommon for a House Bill. Except for highly controversial bills or votes that are expected to be extremely close, few House members listened to the floor debates.* For the waterway bill, as for most of the other issues they voted on every day, the members of the House would have to find out what was at stake from lobbyists, or newspapers, or committee reports, or from asking around among their colleagues until they found somebody who knew what the waterway user charge was all about.

The debates and votes on the House bill turned out to be anticlimactic. A few die-hard barge lobbyists, with the backing of a few diehards in the House, were still working against the imposition of any waterway fee at all. Bedell, Edgar, and three dozen other members, supported by a mild lobbying effort from railroad and environmental groups, argued that the Ullman fuel-tax plan was far too low. Bedell tried hard to enlist the Administration on his side of the struggle. Adams, though, felt obliged to refuse him, because when O'Neill had resolved the blue-slip crisis, Adams had promised to let the Speaker run the show in the House. Consequently, the Administration's only contribution was an enigmatic letter from Adams to House members asking them to vote for the Ullman fuel-tax bill. "The Administration does feel that the recovery level . . . is too low," the letter said, "but will work on the Senate side to increase the recovery level." To Bedell, who had been working to "increase the recovery level" in the House, this missive was the unkindest cut of all. "We've got an expression for that out in Iowa," Bedell observed dryly when he saw Adams' letter. "We call it stabbing your buddy in the back."

The House chamber, a large, sloping room with row after row of brown leather seats banking upward from front to back, looks, when empty, like an elegant amphitheater. When the House is in session, the chamber takes on the appearance, to an observer high in the

---

*This situation changed somewhat beginning with the 96th Congress, when an innovation—closed-circuit television—permitted members to watch the debates in their offices via TV.

galleries, of a human ant farm. People scurry busily to and fro through the aisles, they gather in knots of five or ten for conversation, and only a small number pay attention to the debate that is going on at the front of the room. On October 13, when the floor schedule called for final debate and vote on the Lock and Dam 26/user-charge bill—the closed rule had been approved at a floor vote on October 6—there were about 60 members on the floor, of whom fewer than a dozen seemed to be listening to the speeches pro and con. By the time Berkley Bedell got to the rostrum, the members were restless, and Bedell was interrupted repeatedly by shouts of "Vote! Vote!" from the corners of the chamber. Finally, O'Neill, from the Speaker's chair, called for a vote. The bells signaling a roll call sounded in the House office buildings, and members came pouring onto the floor to signal "aye" or "nay" on the electronic voting machine. When the machine finished its count, the waterway bill had passed by a margin of 331 to 70.

The measure that passed in the House—formally designated H.R.8309—was, to be sure, a watered-down waterway bill. But House approval of the basic concept of a waterway charge seemed, to most of those who had followed the bill, to prove once more the wisdom of Pete Domenici's "hostage" strategy—linking the waterway toll to a major waterway construction project. There were further skirmishes ahead in the Senate, because the Senate's bill had been left to die, and the Senate would have to act on H.R.8309 as a new bill. But most of the experts in Washington expected the user charge to emerge from the Senate with little difficulty.

As often happens, the experts were wrong. In the months to come, the struggle over a waterway user charge would become more difficult than ever. The trouble stemmed from a reaction that set in against the user-charge idea when it became clear that the House would approve the concept. This might have been called a "grass-roots reaction" against the Washington establishment—except that this reaction welled up on the rivers, among the hard-working breed of people who ran the barges and who were beginning to sense that, if they didn't do something, Congress was about to change their way of life.

13

On the River

The muddy Mississippi bends gently westward around the little town of Hickman, Kentucky, and the towboat *Bernard G.*, pushing a nest of barges downstream to New Orleans, throttles back to take the turn. The throbbing of her two huge diesel engines dies away, and in the sudden silence that falls over boat and river a passenger in *Bernard G.*'s pilot house can almost hear Huckleberry Finn out there somewhere on his raft, carrying on even now about "the *goldurndest* river a body ever see." At first glance, the Mississippi today seems to be the same isolated natural wonder that won the heart of Huck Finn. Although *Bernard G.*'s travels upstream and down take her through the very heart of the United States, the boat can go for hours without sighting a village, whole days without passing under a bridge. For long stretches, the milewide river is flanked by nothing but virgin forests and high sand bluffs. To the newcomer, the Mississippi still looks like the "magnificent untamed torrent" that Mark Twain knew.

"New people always talk like that," Ken Bain, *Bernard G.*'s burly, blunt-spoken captain, says to a visitor who has come to ride the boat for a few days while the user-charge bill is pending in the House. "We get passengers—city people—they come aboard for a couple of days to see what it's like, and right away they start talking about Huckleberry Finn. We don't talk about that stuff. To us, the river is just a highway."

Bain's point is well taken. As the crew of *Bernard G.* know, the

"Father of the Waters" is no longer the same rampaging river that Mark Twain had glorified a century before. Decades of damming, diking, and dredging by the Corps of Engineers have harnessed the Mississippi, making it a reliable, predictable highway for the barge lines that move enormous quantities of freight between Minneapolis and New Orleans. At almost every turn, the Army has put in a dike or jetty to direct the current and keep the towboats and their barges in midstream. A fleet of Army workboats is continually dredging a passable channel along the shifting river bottom. To mark the channel, the Coast Guard maintains lights and buoys every quarter-mile or so along the Mississippi's 1,000-mile course. Where dredging is not enough, the Corps has erected immense dams to deepen the river; each dam requires locks to let the barges pass.

The government's multibillion-dollar investment in the Mississippi—and 23,000 miles of other inland waterways—has created a livelihood for Ken Bain and his shipmates on *Bernard G.* and for tens of thousands of crew members on other boats. The barge industry, in turn, has spawned a booming service industry of ports and shipyards. The Mississippi and other river highways are dotted with cities whose economic tides rise and fall with barge traffic. "The city of St. Louis is located where it is for only one reason," Danforth had said during the Senate debate on S.790, and, while that assertion was dismissed in Washington as standard political hyperbole, on the river it is considered a simple statement of fact.

In Washington, the user-charge bill is generally viewed as a political and parliamentary coup for Pete Domenici and Jimmy Carter. On the river, though, S.790 is seen as a dagger in the back. A Congress that has always been generous in funding waterways development is suddenly trying to change the rules. That perception, growing gradually during the summer and fall, has created a feeling among the river people that the user-charge legislation has to be stopped. "We have to fight this," says Bob Gardner, the commodore of the towboat fleet maintained by the Alter Company, the Iowa firm that owns *Bernard G.* "For years we've been doing a job out here —hauling grain—and we don't do it bad when people leave us alone. This year, all of a sudden, we're in this political volleyball game with a bunch of people who don't understand the river or our business. Barging is slow, but it's reliable, and it's cheap. That's where we get our business. If Washington puts a toll on us, we've got to raise our rates. And then all that freight I'm pushing is going to start moving by train. We've got an investment of $2.3 million in *Bernard G.*, and she isn't going to look very good sitting in some backwater all year."

On the river, though, *Bernard G.* (the boat's name was the brain-child of Alter's president, Bernard Goldstein) is a smart-looking craft. A gleaming white boat with yellow trim, she looks like a four-tiered rectangular wedding cake with a forest of antennae sprouting from the top layer. The boat is 145 feet long and 40 feet wide, about average for Mississippi River towboats. Her draft is only 9 feet—any more and she could not traverse the 29 pools that constitute the upper Mississippi. The top deck of the floating cake is the "pilot house"—what a seagoing sailor would call the "bridge." Stacked beneath it are three more enclosed decks, each slightly bigger than the one above, housing crew and guest quarters, a galley and dining room, and various storage lockers. The lowest deck is essentially one big engine room, holding the two thundering Detroit Diesel engines that send a never-ending shudder through the spine of the boat (at full power, the crew members' coffee vibrates right out of the cups).

The 5,600-horsepower diesels make *Bernard G.* one of the most overpowered 145-footers that ever took to water. But the power, of course, is not there for the towboat. It is there to push the "tow." In the barge business, terminology is backward. Although the riverboats are called "towboats," they don't tow. They push the barges ahead of them. But the nest of barges that is pushed is called the "tow."

The tow assembled for this typical downstream passage by *Bernard G.* is about average, the crew members say. There are 21 barges, strung together in a four-by-five block (with the extra barge nosing ahead out front) that covers five acres of river. Each barge is about the size of a two-story, ten-unit apartment building, with about 8 feet of its bulk below the waterline and another 10 feet above. The barges are grain hoppers, for the most part, carrying Midwestern corn and soybeans bound for rendezvous in New Orleans with a European freighter, but there are some molasses and tallow tanks along as well. In total, *Bernard G.* is pushing about 30,000 tons of freight on this one trip; it would take three 100-car trains, or 1,200 big trucks, to move as much.

The individual barges are bound tightly together by iron cobwebs of 1½-inch cables wound in intricate networks around each corner of the barge. A separate set of cables, their tautness maintained by a pair of big winches, ties the tow to the front of *Bernard G.* The ties that bind the barges will burst if bound too tightly, or give way if not held taut enough. To guard against either, deckhands roam about the tow at all times, kicking and pulling at the lines in the same boat-man's ballet that Huck Finn watched at night from his raft.

Four decks above the tow, the *Bernard G.*'s pilot house looks more like something from *Star Trek* than from Mark Twain. Dials glow; warning lights blink; two large radar screens bathe the pilot's face in an eerie green glow. The pilot, scanning the digital readouts from two sonar units that read the river's depth, steers not with the classic multispoked wooden wheel but with a stainless-steel tiller linked by hydraulic drive to the rudders astern.

Bernard G. has two pilots—Captain Bain and his relief, John McNeil—who drive the boat in alternating six-hour shifts, around the clock. The two men reflect two sharply different styles of piloting. McNeil, a perfect country gentleman from Greenville, Mississippi, is the tortoise. When the Corps of Engineers' intricately detailed navigation chart shows a sharp curve coming, he cuts the engines a half-mile upstream, letting the current carry boat and tow gently around the turn. Bain, a hot-rodder from Savannah, Tennessee, prefers to barrel into the turns at full speed (about 11 miles per hour), wrenching the pneumatic throttle from "full ahead" to "full astern" to keep the unwieldy chain of barges from piling over a bank or sandbar. Under either man, though, the pilot house has an air of easy nonchalance, like a suburban family out for a Sunday drive. The difference is that this "car" has a hood longer than three football fields jutting out beyond the windshield. Where the river is wide and the curves easy, it seems simple enough to keep the long tow in line. Around the sharp bends, though, driving a riverboat is like pushing the Washington Monument up a winding road ahead of the family station wagon—with no brakes.

With the prodigious weight of the tow up ahead, it would take *Bernard G.* well over a mile to come to a stop on its downstream voyage. This sobering fact means that the pilots have to keep talking continuously into their CB radios to let the boats ahead know they are coming and to inform those behind of what is in store. Each time they approach another boat and tow, they establish ad hoc rules of the road by radio to avoid a collision.

"I'm coming up along the bend at Hickman, Cap'n," Bain says to the pilot of the boat heading straight at him about a mile up ahead. "Which side you want to take?"

"Don't make no never mind to me, Cap'n," the answer comes. "Why don't you stay on the Kentucky bank, and I'll take her over to the Missouri side?"

"Sounds good, Cap'n. Now you got two more good-size tows coming right after me."

The casual chatter on the airwaves makes the whole river seem like a big family, and in some ways it is. The boat crews almost all share the same Southern country upbringing, they are common stock in a common business, and they all seem to feel an affinity for every boat and crew member on the river. The sense of family is particularly strong within the crew of *Bernard G.*, who live together on the little boat for 30 days at a time or more. Although the boat is regularly in such ports as St. Louis and New Orleans, these sailors get no liberty. *Bernard G.* stops only long enough to drop one tow and pick up another. In port or on the river, the crew members work seven days a week, two six-hour shifts each day. Each six-hour shift includes a driver (either Bain or McNeil), an engineer to watch the diesels, and three deckhands working the tow. The eleventh crew member, the only woman aboard, is the boat's cook, nurse, and den mother, Janie Devers, a Tennessee belle who serves up a gargantuan banquet of country food at each change of the watch.

The crew members generally work 30 days on the boat and then take 15 or 20 days off, so they are actually on the job only seven to nine months a year. For that, a beginning deckhand can expect to earn $10,000 to $12,000 annually. A captain's pay approaches $30,000, sometimes more. But the work is exhausting.

When a six-hour watch is finished, the crew of *Bernard G.* sit in Janie's air-conditioned galley for an hour or more, sipping Dr. Pepper and regaining their strength. The talk around the galley table is half river jargon and half country stories about the farms back home. Bain, the captain, is a constant topic, for he apparently drives even less delicately at home than he does in *Bernard G.*'s pilot house. "I remember the week Kenny cracked up his wife's car one night and his own the next," laughs the engineer, James Porter, in his easy drawl. "Then he goes and rents another, and damn if that one doesn't end up a wreck, too."

The boatmen are an independent breed, distrustful of big business and big government in equal proportions, and in normal times there is little talk of politics aboard *Bernard G.* But S.790 has changed that. On the bulletin board above the color television in the crew's lounge is a letter from a barge-industry association. "Dear Captain," it says. "You are aware, I'm sure, that the river industry is in real trouble. The railroads and the environmentalists are doing a job on us. . . . We need money. Our expenses with a law firm in Washington and the American Inland Waterways Committee run about $2,500 per month, and may get higher. Can you and your crew help?" Most of the crew on *Bernard G.* have sent in something to help. "I don't know how the thing got as far as it has got," Porter, the engineer, says with a shake of the head. "But I know my job's in trouble if they put a tax on this barge. We burn up 49,000 gallons of diesel fuel in a week. Now who's going to pay a tax on that? We got to get working now to stop this thing."

Up in the pilot house, John McNeil, the Mississippi gentleman, agrees. "I know it's wrong, that's what I know," McNeil says quietly. "It's like you go over here to some little stream and catch you a mess of fish. Then that fellow comes up and says, 'You got to pay me for those fish.' It's not right. It ain't the idea of paying the $3. It's the idea of paying for a river. It's not right."

14

Unlikely Allies

It took a while for the reaction from *Bernard G.* and from other scattered elements of the water-freight industry to filter back to the Washington offices of the industry associations and their numerous lobbyists, but eventually the message did get through. By the fall of 1977, there was a noticeable stiffening of the backbone among the barge lobbyists in Washington. This metamorphosis came too late to make any difference in the House, where H.R.8309 was gliding along the path Tip O'Neill had cleared for it. But by the time O'Neill's compromise bill passed the House, and the waterway fight moved back to the Senate, there was a determination within the barge community to try, once more, to pass a Lock and Dam 26 authorization without any user charge attached to it. "A lot of us have the feeling," Ron Schrader, one of the chief barge lobbyists, explained a few days after the House vote, "that the veto business is a phony. We think the President will sign a lock and dam bill whether or not he gets a tax with it."

This feeling was partly wishful thinking, but it stemmed in part from the actions of Jimmy Carter himself. During his first months in the White House, Carter had shocked Congress by compiling a "hit list" of proposed waterway projects that he considered "wasteful and unjustified." He had threatened, at least implicitly, to veto authorization bills for projects on the hit list. This kind of interference in an area that had always been Congress' special preserve was unprecedented, and while Carter did have the support of many junior members of Congress who were not yet accustomed to the pork-barrel ethic, the hit list was attacked by the leadership in both houses —even by Tip O'Neill. Eventually, Congress passed an authorization bill funding most of the projects Carter had challenged. The White House staff urged Carter to veto, but the President, under intense pressure from O'Neill, signed the bill into law. That concession —which Carter subsequently called the most serious mistake of his first year in office—was widely viewed as a retreat. It necessarily undermined the credibility of the veto threat aimed at Lock and Dam 26, and thus strengthened the barge lines' resolve.

One of the first people in Congress to notice the barge lines' tough new frame of mind was Russell Long. Long had been delighted with the 6-cent fuel-tax bill passed by the House, and he expected H.R.8309 to pave the way for a quick and easy final resolution of the whole controversy in the Senate. As Long figured things, the Senate would probably amend the House bill somewhat, doubling or tripling the size of the tax. When the House and Senate versions of the bill went to conference, Long thought, the conferees would split the difference and produce a bill that authorized Lock and Dam 26 and imposed a waterway fee of about 10 cents per gallon. To Long, who was, above all else, a pragmatist, that result was the best the barge lines could realistically hope for—and it would be a bargain, he told them. After all, Long explained in a meeting with the barge lobbyists in mid-October, the bill the Senate passed, S.790, would have cost the industry more than $350 million annually; a 10-cent fuel tax would cost less than a quarter of that.

But the barge lines weren't buying. When the Senate took up the issue again, they told Long, the barge lobbyists would have no part in any compromise. They would not support a bill costing even one penny more than the House's mild tax would raise. Indeed, they might work in the Senate to scrub the user charge altogether—and they would expect Russell Long's help if they chose that course. The Senator was not at all pleased. "I'm likely to get a little perturbed with these fellows," he said a few days after his session with the lobbyists. "There comes a time when you have to get realistic and give way an inch or two. That's how legislating works. But those barge boys—they're saying they ain't going to move at all."

At the same time, the supporters of the waterway charge were toughening their position as well. Even before the House completed action on H.R.8309, Domenici put out a press release stating that the

6-cent fuel tax in that bill was "totally inadequate," because the tax level was too low and the legislation had no capital-recovery mechanism. Brock Adams agreed. As soon as the House had finished its work on the bill, Adams sent a letter to the Senate warning that the President would not sign a bill that had nothing more than the House's 6-cent fuel tax. The Lock and Dam 26 authorization would be vetoed, Adams wrote, unless the Senate, in its consideration of H.R.8309, added a "substantial" waterway charge. What would be "substantial" was left unsaid—except for the observation that the House bill was not substantial enough.

By Friday, October 13, accordingly—when three House clerks formally delivered a copy of the House-passed legislation to the Senate—both sides were in the mood to fight. Because S.790 had been shelved when it reached the House, the Senate had to start all over again on the waterway legislation. Normally, a House-passed bill would be treated in the Senate just like a piece of newly intro-duced legislation—it would be referred to the appropriate commit-tee. H.R.8309, containing a water construction authorization and a tax provision, should have been jointly referred to the Public Works Committee and to Russell Long's Finance Committee. Domenici, of course, wanted to keep the measure out of Long's hands, so he in-voked an obscure provision in the rules under which Legislation transmitted from the House can be held at the Senate floor without referral to a committee. Long was unfazed. Even if he didn't have jurisdiction over a particular bill, he said, he was still a committee chairman, and he could call a hearing on "the general subject of waterway taxes"—which he promptly did. After a one-day hearing on this "general subject," the Finance Committee agreed that the Senate should accept a 6-cent tax plan phased in over a period of years; in other words, the committee recommended that the Senate accept H.R.8309 as the House passed it, with no capital-recovery provision.

Once this initial flurry of maneuvering was over, however, H.R.8309's progress came to a halt. With both supporters and oppo-nents of the user charge determined to stand firm, the Senate was effectively stalemated on the issue. Early in November, Robert C. Byrd, the Majority Leader, approached Long and Domenici about scheduling a new Senate vote—a vote that would let Senators decide among three options: the stiff, S.790-style user charge the Senate had passed, the mild, H.R.8309-style charge the House had approved, or no charge at all. Long and Domenici both demurred. Since neither man was sure he had the votes to prevail, neither was anxious to take the matter to the floor. Week after week Byrd tried to schedule a vote, and week after week the two protagonists came up with excuses for delaying it again. The matter dragged on and on, and in late December, when Congress finally recessed for the year-end holidays, the waterway user charge bill was still in the "pending" column.

When the members of Congress returned to Washington in mid-January 1978 to begin the 95th Congress' second session, the whole Senate—and for that matter, the whole of Washington—was buzzing about the crucial waterway vote coming up. But it was not the user-charge bill that people were talking about; the subject was the Panama Canal, and the treaties Jimmy Carter had negotiated ceding that waterway to the government of Panama. The Senate vote on ratification was to be the most serious test yet of Carter's foreign policy, and the Senators were determined to make the treaties the subject of a major debate. From the day the treaties came to the floor, in early February, until the vote on the final treaty three months later (the pacts were approved by a one-vote margin), Panama was the only major issue on the Senate floor. The waterway user charge had to wait in line with numerous other bills backed up on the calendar.

For all its political and diplomatic significance, though, the Senate debate on Panama was a plodding affair, and it left the Senators —few of whom actually listened to their colleagues' speeches—a good deal of time to work on other issues. All through the spring, Long and Domenici and their staff aides, with assorted kibitzers from the executive branch and from lobby groups on both sides of the issue, were engaged in almost continuous negotiations, searching for a compromise version of the user-charge/Lock and Dam 26 bill. The two Senators had their differences, of course, but they also discovered that they had some points of agreement. In light of the Senate vote on S.790, Long was willing to admit that some level of user charge would be enacted. In light of the House action, Domenici was willing to admit that he would have trouble passing the stringent charge incorporated in S.790. Accordingly, each man was willing to give in—up to a point.

But there were two obstacles to agreement.

First, there was a basic difference of opinion on the capital-recovery concept. For Domenici, linkage between the government's spending on waterways and the charge imposed on waterway users was an essential element of any user-charge bill. Long was reluctant

to go along; a linkage requirement, he said, would violate his personal conviction that tax rates should be set by Congress, rather than by
a formula in the hands of the executive branch.

The second problem was kibitzers. Both Long and Domenici were
representing multifaceted constituencies, and the infighting among
these groups made it almost impossible for the Senators to settle
anything. On the anti-user-charge front, Long, to his growing consternation, was faced with an ever-changing roster of lobbyists representing separate factions of the water-freight industry. Some were
willing to compromise with Domenici; some told Long to stand firm
on the House bill, and some argued for a lock and dam bill untainted
by any user charge. On Domenici's side, things were even more
complicated. A dissident group of rail lobbyists led by Judy Durrand,
a tough, no-nonsense vice president of the Missouri–Pacific Railroad, had grown dissatisfied with Joe Feeney's leadership and had
set up their own lobbying organization. The Durrand faction gave
Domenici leeway to negotiate a compromise bill; Feeney and his
allies in the environmental movement, though, kept telling the Senator not to retreat an inch from the provisions of S.790.

Long and Domenici, meanwhile, had other bills to worry about—
Long, particularly, seemed to be at the center of every major legislative battle on the Hill—and, when the two Senators were engaged
in other business, the kibitzers carried on by themselves. The principal negotiators on Domenici's side were Brayman, Sue Williams of
the Transportation Department, and Brent Blackwelder, one of the
environmentalists allied with Feeney. The barge lines had a long list
of negotiators, all theoretically of equal status, but by early spring
one had clearly emerged as more equal than the rest: Louis Susman,
the coarse, cocky, curly-haired lawyer from St. Louis who ran the ad
hoc committee the barge interests had set up specifically to deal with
the user-charge problem. Susman had farmed out the lobbying work
on the bill to Smathers and other Washington types, but he personally took over the negotiations—because negotiating was his forte. He
had honed the skill in his role as counsel to the St. Louis Cardinals, a
job that required him, each spring, to battle over contract demands
with some of America's highest-priced athletic talent.

For the first three months of 1978, Susman's life turned into one
continuous shuttle between the Cardinals' Florida training camp and
Capitol Hill. "Ballplayers, Senators—there's really not all that much
difference," Susman observed during one of his stops in Washington.
"In both cases, I'm just trying to make sure my clients don't pay a
penny more than they have to." Susman's chief technique—in

Washington, at least—was to take a tough initial position and stick to it. "That guy Susman could drive you crazy," Brayman complained. "We put something on the table, and all the barge guys kind of nod and look interested, and then we get the word from Susman, and it's always 'No dice.'"

By the end of the Panama Canal debate, consequently, Russell Long and Pete Domenici were not much closer to agreement than they had been six months before. The lack of progress caused considerable concern in the Senate. Byrd, the keeper of the schedule, was worried that, if he brought the waterway bill to the floor, the opposing sides would debate it for weeks, putting a serious crimp in his plans to adjourn early in the fall so that Senators could go home to campaign. Gravel and Stevenson began to worry that no agreement would be reached—meaning no lock and dam authorization in the 95th Congress. Since committee and floor votes from one Congress cannot be carried over to the next, the waterway bill would then have to start all over again in both houses in the 96th Congress. Gravel, who had unhappy visions of the whole imbroglio coming back anew to his subcommittee, was furious. "Those damn guys, Pete and Russell, they're like a pair of Sumo wrestlers," Gravel said. "They dance around outside the ring throwing salt in the air, but they're both afraid to get in the ring—because they both think they're going to lose."

In addition, a large number of Senators who had no particular interest in the user charge or the Alton dam were worried, too. In each Congress, the Public Works Committee designates a single bill as the omnibus legislation to be the vehicle for waterway pork-barrel projects; when H.R.8309 came over from the House, Jennings Randolph, the Public Works chairman, picked it to be the pork-barrel vehicle for the 95th Congress. By April 1978, as a result, more than 60 amendments to H.R.8309 had been introduced, each authorizing a project that was important to at least one Senator. But no one knew when, or even if, the vehicle would come to the floor.

The most concerned figure of all, though, was Brock Adams. The spring of 1978 had not been propitious for the Secretary of Transportation. In articles reviewing the first year of the Carter Administration, two major newspapers had identified him as the least effective member of Jimmy Carter's cabinet—and the least respected by the White House staff. Whether or not this assessment was fair, it was the kind of report that could become self-fulfilling. If the politicians and corporate executives with whom Adams dealt in his job believed that he was out of favor at the White House, they would be less willing to defer to his judgment—and that, over time, would make him ineffective. This very problem, in fact, was threatening to crop up on the waterway bill. Ever since Adams had sent his vague letter threatening a veto if the Senate did not approve a "substantial" waterway charge, a lot of Senators—good Democrats like Long, Stevenson, and Magnuson—had been telling their colleagues that the Secretary's threat was a hollow bluff. Long, who had talked to Carter personally about the user-charge question late in 1977, told the other Senators that he came away with the impression that Carter might sign a lock and dam bill even with the House's minimal user charge— despite Brock Adams' threat to the contrary. When this story started passing through the Senate, Adams received an urgent call from an old friend of his, Senator Gaylord Nelson, the Wisconsin Democrat. "You've got a problem here, Brock," Nelson said. "If we pass that House bill, and Carter doesn't veto, your credibility is going to be mincemeat around here."

To make matters worse, Adams was getting conflicting signals on the issue from the White House staff. Frank Moore, the President's chief lobbyist, who had to deal with Russell Long on a lot of legislation more important than any barge bill, wanted Carter to give in. "If we let Russell win this one," Moore told Adams, "he'll owe us a favor on the energy bill or welfare reform, where we really need him," On the other hand, Stuart Eizenstat, Carter's domestic issues expert, was taking the hardest possible line in favor of a veto.

Faced with this clear split among the President's advisers, Adams finally decided that his only recourse was to take the question directly to the President. But that was something more easily decided than done. It was not that easy, even if you were Secretary of Transportation, to get in to see the President at a time when the White House was wrapped up in the fate of the Panama Canal treaties. Finally, Adams collared Carter in a doorway one morning after a staff meeting at the White House and laid out the situation. Carter understood immediately what the problem was and assured Adams that something would be done.

A few hours later, something was. A messenger from the White House showed up in Adams' office that afternoon bearing a brief note on White House letterhead, signed by Richard G. Hutcheson III, a young aide who bore the title "Presidential Staff Secretary"—a glorified term for Chief Paper Shuffler. "Let our position be clearly known," Hutcheson quoted Carter as saying, "including possibility of veto." It wasn't everything Adams might have hoped for—a message over the President's personal signature would have had more punch on Capitol Hill—but the Secretary figured it was probably enough. The Hutcheson memo was quickly copied and dispatched to the Senate.

All this time the negotiations were continuing, week after fruitless week. By the middle of April, with Susman still rejecting each new Domenici proposal and Brayman finding something unacceptable about each new idea from the barge side, Domenici finally broke off the talks altogether, and Brayman announced to the negotiators on both sides that the Senator was going to ask Byrd to schedule a vote early in May, compromise or no compromise. This development worried the barge lobby, which assumed that their chief adversary had to have a trick up his sleeve somewhere. "Senator Domenici might pull some last-minute voting ploy," Harry Cook warned in a memorandum to his fellow bargemen. "Admittedly, he is crafty and resourceful. And he won last June."

Cook, of course, was dead right. Domenici had indeed changed tactics. If he couldn't negotiate with Russell Long and the barge lobby, Domenici decided, he would find somebody else to deal with.

Adams, who had been making his own soundings in the Senate, suggested to Domenici that he might find an ally in Adlai Stevenson. On the surface, this seemed impossible; Stevenson, after all, had been the floor manager of the anti-user-charge position when S.790 was on the Senate floor. But, as Adams knew, Stevenson's main interest was in passing the authorization for Lock and Dam 26, the most important public-works project in his home state. Whatever he might have thought about a user charge before, Stevenson was now ready to pay the price to get the Alton project approved. Domenici, for his part, had no objection to authorizing the lock and dam, if he could get a user charge in the bargain. So the erstwhile adversaries got together, and in a matter of days they had come up with a jointly acceptable legislative package.

Before the new Stevenson–Domenici bill could go to the floor, however, both Senators insisted that Brock Adams produce a clear, undeniable commitment of Presidential support—something more impressive than a brief memo from a junior White House functionary. Adams dutifully went back to the White House, and, with Eizen-

stat's help, convinced Frank Moore that this was, after all, an issue
that warranted an explicit veto threat. Late in April, Adams, Eizenstat, and Moore all signed a memo to the President recommending
full White House support for the Stevenson–Domenici proposal.

"We are reluctant to oppose Senator Long in a floor fight," the
memo said. But, it added, "we have little to lose by backing the
Stevenson–Domenici substitute. If we win . . . your leadership will
have visibly and decisively affected the outcome. If we lose, you will
be in the position of having given fair warning of your intentions to
veto." This reasoning was good enough for Carter, who personally
liked the strategy of holding Lock and Dam 26 a hostage to the waterway fee. Late in April he called Adams and gave the go-ahead for a
tough new veto letter. With the assurance of White House backing,
Stevenson and Domenici called a joint press conference to announce
their new bill.

The Democrat from Illinois and the Republican from New Mexico
seemed an unlikely team as they came into the Senate press gallery
on May Day of 1978 to announce their plan. Stevenson, a tall, bald-
ing, immaculately dressed figure with an almost Victorian air of
aloofness, stood stiffly erect and spoke in formal legislative tones.
Domenici, an easygoing fellow with dandruff on his shoulders and a
big splotch of ink on his shirt pocket, slouched against the wall and
talked casually through a cloud of cigarette smoke. The joint proposal they described was a combination of parts of S.790 and parts of
H.R.8309. Their bill would impose a fuel tax, starting at 4 cents per
gallon and increasing gradually to 12 cents. But it would also include
a separate fee system in addition to the tax—a system that would
recover a fixed percentage of the government's waterway expenditures each year. In addition, of course, the Stevenson–Domenici bill
would authorize Lock and Dam 26.

As the two Senators distributed printed copies of their new plan,
they also passed out copies of the new Brock Adams letter that gave
their plan its teeth. The message was the most explicit statement yet
of the hostage strategy: The Stevenson–Domenici waterway fee was
the "minimum" Jimmy Carter would accept, the letter said. "The
President," Adams wrote, "will not sign legislation authorizing a
new lock and dam at Alton, Illinois, unless it . . . would provide for
some capital cost recovery."

The reporters had two questions.

"When will you take this bill to the floor?" somebody asked.

Domenici answered in a voice that rang with confidence. "We're ready any time," he said. "We've asked the majority leader to schedule a vote this week—maybe as soon as the third [of May]."

"And do you think you'll win?" another reporter asked.

"Well, let's put it this way," Stevenson responded, sounding a little less confident than his new ally. "Senator Domenici won last time, and this time he's got at least one more vote. He's got me."

15

Head to Head—Again

On June 22, 1977, when the waterway user charge had reached the Senate floor for the first time, the head counters for the various lobbying groups had been uncertain about the Senate's collective attitude toward the issue. On May 3, 1978—when the Stevenson–Domenici compact brought the user charge back to the floor a second time—the head counters were utterly mystified. Their surveys of the 100 Senators were giving them a fairly clear picture of what the vote would be—but the picture didn't make sense. Most of the head counts indicated that Domenici and Stevenson (and Jimmy Carter along with them) were going to lose.

On paper, that result seemed almost impossible. As Stevenson had pointed out at the press conference, the pro-user-charge position should have been stronger than it was when S.790 passed the Senate, because Domenici had now won over one of S.790's chief opponents. Moreover, the Stevenson–Domenici user-charge plan was considerably milder than the fairly stringent fee structure encompassed in S.790; any Senator who had been willing to vote for S.790, it seemed reasonable to assume, would find the new bill acceptable, and some who had not been willing to accept the S.790 user charge might go along with the new, milder version. Finally, Domenici's basic "hostage" strategy was still alive—and, indeed, more explicit than ever before. For now the President had made it clear that it would take no less than the Stevenson–Domenici bill, including the capital-recovery provision, to get him to sign an authorization bill for Lock and Dam 26.

However strong the user charge's chances looked on paper, however, there were serious problems facing the bill in the Senate. Domenici was still a junior Republican going up against senior members of the majority party. In that regard, the alliance with Stevenson was not much help. The Senator from Illinois had no clout to speak of within his party; a loner in the Senate, he had never been very good at twisting arms to get his way. "If we picked up any votes by getting Adlai aboard," complained Sue Williams, the Transportation Department head counter, the day before the floor vote, "I haven't been able to find them." The clout remained with Long and the other river-state Democrats.

When word got out that Domenici and Stevenson had forged an alliance, Long met with a group of barge lobbyists to develop a line of defense to this surprising new offensive. Long stipulated at the outset that the barge lines were going to have to accept some waterway fee in order to win the Alton authorization; the House vote had settled that question once and for all. But Long promised he would work to hold the fee as low as it could possibly be. The Senator and the lobbyists agreed quickly that they would fight to the end against any capital-recovery mechanism—that is, any formula that would increase the fee when government costs increased—since Long opposed the idea out of principle and the barge lobbyists were afraid it would squelch their plans for some major new waterway projects. Instead, it was agreed, the barge industry would support a Long amendment establishing a fuel tax—a tax twice as high as the tax in the House bill. That would let the House–Senate conferees compromise on a tax level somewhere in the middle.

When Long formally introduced his fuel-tax plan on May 2, Brayman went over to the Senate floor to get a copy, and he saw immediately that it was an ingenious response to the Stevenson–Domenici proposal. The fuel tax Long proposed—starting at 4 cents per gallon and increasing gradually to 12 cents—was precisely the level in the Stevenson–Domenici bill. "He's got everything we've got," Brayman said, "except capital recovery. We know that that's the most important thing in the bill, but most guys won't know that. Russell's going to tell everybody that his bill is almost the same as ours."

With the battle lines clearly drawn, the two sides launched intensive last-minute lobbying campaigns. For the most part, the lobbyists and their arguments were nearly the same as they had been a year earlier, when S.790 was before the Senate. For this second vote, however, the barge lobbyists had significant assistance from a new flank—the national farm lobbies. As the farm groups saw it, farmers would lose in two ways if the Senate passed a high waterway fee: Shipping rates would go up immediately for farmers who shipped their crops to market by barge, and that would ease the competitive pressure on railroads, leading eventually to rate increases for rail-carried farm products as well. The farm lobbyists focused on farm-state Senators who had supported Domenici on S.790. They won three outright converts—Republican Robert J. Dole, of Kansas; Democrat George McGovern, of South Dakota; and Republican Clifford P. Hansen, of Wyoming—and elicited a "maybe" from Democrat Birch Bayh, of Indiana.

Another factor undermining Domenici's position was the impending 1978 election. The thought of a reelection contest had been a fairly remote concern in June 1977, when S.790 was before the Senate, but now, in May 1978, it was a priority consideration for many Senators. Baker, the minority leader, who had bucked the waterway interests in his state to support Domenici on S.790, now said that he would have to vote against the Stevenson–Domenici plan. It was simply too risky for a Senator from Tennessee to vote against the water-freight industry six months before his seat would be on the line. Similarly, Clifford P. Case, a New Jersey Republican who had a tough GOP primary coming up, told Domenici apologetically the day before the vote that he could not support him this time. The New Jersey AFL–CIO had endorsed Case's bid for a new term, and in return the Senator felt obliged to go along with the union's opposition to any waterway fee that included a capital-recovery mechanism.

Election-year politics, however, gave Domenici one vote he had lost the year before. Percy, the Illinois Republican, had a tough reelection race, and his opponent was sharply critical of Percy's transparent effort to please both sides by his vote on S.790. Percy decided that the safest thing to do was to side with his colleague from Illinois, and so he promised to vote for the Stevenson–Domenici bill. That gain, though, was offset by a diplomatic blunder on Domenici's part. A few days before the waterway bill came up, Domenici had delivered a strong floor speech criticizing one of Mike Gravel's pet legislative projects. Gravel was livid: "You just lost me on that user charge, Pete," he snapped, and Domenici was powerless to win him back.

Even the calendar seemed to be working against Domenici and

Stevenson. As soon as the pair had reached a general agreement, they had told Byrd, the majority leader, that they were ready for a vote. When Long said that he was ready, too, Byrd scheduled the vote for the first available day—Tuesday, May 3. But that was not an ordinary day. The third of May had been designated "Sun Day" by environmental groups promoting greater development of solar-energy facilities (it was a lucky choice because the day turned out to be warm and bright across the country), and pro-solar demonstrations had been scheduled in cities around the nation. Among the speakers scheduled at several of the demonstrations were members of the Senate. Since the Senators invited to address Sun Day rallies were environmentally minded individuals—the kind who would support the stiffest possible waterway fee—Sun Day pulled away from Washington four Senators who had been present and voting on Domenici's side when S.790 had come up.

The most serious problem facing Domenici, however, was that his strongest weapon—the veto threat—was not working. "A lot of guys just don't believe that Carter will veto," Domenici observed unhappily a few hours before the Senate was scheduled to take up the bill. "I've told everybody a dozen times that, without capital recovery, this bill won't get signed. But a lot of guys really believe that Russell's bill will be good enough to get by." This was, of course, the viewpoint that the barge lobbyists were spreading—that Long's version of the waterway fee was enough to convince Carter to sign the Lock and Dam 26 authorization.

There were several reasons for this refusal to believe the President's warning. As Brayman had predicted, many Senators failed to perceive the difference in principle between a flat-rate tax on water freight and a capital-recovery system linking the tax to the government's costs. Thus, they could not comprehend why Carter would insist on capital recovery. Further, many Senators thought it unlikely that Carter would take a step as drastic as a veto on this relatively minor issue. "He's got most of his legislative program still pending up here," Danforth, the Missouri Republican, kept telling his colleagues. "There's no way he's going to go to the mat with us on this bill."

By the morning of May 3, accordingly, Domenici and his allies knew they were in trouble. After an urgent plea from Domenici, Adams put aside all his other business and spent the whole day trying to reach wavering Senators. Adams scored with Bayh, the Indiana Democrat who was being pressured by the farmers. The Secretary reminded the Senator that his department was just about to act on a huge grant application from Indianapolis for a new mass-transit system. Adams made neither threats nor promises; he didn't have to. Bayh, who badly wanted his state to get its grant, agreed to vote with Domenici. But most of the other Senators Adams talked to were less responsive. At noon, with the Senate debate due to begin in two hours, Adams concluded that the situation demanded heavy artillery—so he called the White House to urge that Carter himself start lobbying.

The President, as it happened, was in a perfect position to help. He was scheduled to speak at a Sun Day rally that afternoon in Colorado. That meant a three-hour midday flight from Washington, and Carter said he would be glad to use the time calling Senators on *Air Force One*'s radio telephone. Soon after he was airborne, Carter got in touch with Jennings Randolph, the West Virginian who had supported Domenici on S.790, but who seemed to be moving to Long's side now. The President gently reminded Randolph of his promise to campaign for Randolph's reelection; by the time the conversation ended, Carter had agreed to make, not one, but two campaign swings to West Virginia, and Randolph had agreed to vote the President's way on the user charge. Carter struck out, though, with Randolph's colleague, Robert Byrd. Byrd said simply that he had given Long a commitment and could not go back on it. Carter's longest conversation was with Muriel Humphrey, who had been appointed to the Senate in January after the death of her husband. Muriel Humphrey had told all the head counters that she was "undecided." At the end of his talk with her, though, Carter called Adams to report that he had received a Humphrey commitment for the Domenici–Stevenson bill.

Despite the tight lobbying battle surrounding it, the floor debate on the Domenici–Stevenson proposal was a desultory affair. The arguments had all been made countless times before. The issue at stake—capital recovery or no capital recovery—was one that most Senators found uninteresting. The most exciting moment came when Long and Domenici flipped a coin to decide whose version of the waterway bill would come up for a vote first. Domenici won, and at 5:55 in the afternoon the Senate bell rang to signal the start of a roll-call vote on the Stevenson-Domenici proposal.

Under Senate rules, members have 15 minutes from the time the first bell rings to get to the floor and cast their votes. In practice, though, a roll call usually takes closer to half an hour, because so many Senators straggle in during the last few minutes that their votes cannot be recorded right away. On this vote, however, it took only 5 minutes to see which way the Senate was going to go. Muriel Humphrey was among the first Senators to vote, and, despite whatever commitment she might have made to the President, she voted "nay"— a vote against Stevenson–Domenici. A minute later, her Minnesota colleague, Democrat Wendell R. Anderson, who followed her lead on almost every issue, came in to cast his "nay." Dole, McGovern, Hansen, and a string of other farm-state members cast "nay" votes as well. Birch Bayh, Charles Percy, and Jennings Randolph voted "aye," as promised; Howard Baker, Clifford Case, Mike Gravel, and Robert Byrd all voted "nay." There were enough Democrats who wanted to be loyal to the President, and enough Republicans who wanted to stick with Domenici, to make the vote close. But when the roll call was finished, the "nays" had it. The Stevenson–Domenici bill— the only user-charge bill not facing a veto threat—had been defeated, 43 to 47.

With that vote completed, the Senate's consideration of the Long amendment was merely a formality. When Long's measure came up for a vote a few minutes later, it passed by a margin of 88 to 2. Long was gracious in victory. "I want to make it clear that the real winner today is not the Senator from Louisiana," the Senator from Louisiana told the Senate. "The Senator from New Mexico made a battle for the tolls on the waterway or user charges, whatever it may be, and he is the winner. He gets 90 percent of what he wants here." Long's ally, Danforth, chimed in on the same note. "This is a great day for Pete Domenici and a great victory for him," Danforth said. "He has succeeded, by virtue of a singular effort, in reversing about 200 years of history."

But if it was such a great day for the Senator from New Mexico, why was he sitting motionless in his chair with a grim, pained looked on his face? Because Pete Domenici knew that, despite the generous rhetoric, he had lost. Without a capital-recovery provision, the user-charge bill—the bill Domenici had spent two years trying to pass—was almost sure to be killed. "My concern," Domenici said in answer to the tribute from Long, "is that we might not get a bill, because the President has indicated he wants some capital recoupment."

The majority of the Senate, of course, did not share that concern. As the vote made clear, the Senators thought Carter would sign the waterway bill anyway. "We have given him a substantial waterway charge," Danforth said at a barge-line victory celebration a few minutes after the Senate vote. "Most of us don't think he will insist on more."

Jimmy Carter, however, seemed to have a different idea. He was en route home from Colorado when the vote was completed, and Brock Adams called *Air Force One* to deliver the bad news. A few minutes later, Adams invited some reporters into his office to tell them what Carter had said. As Adams related it, the President had been short and to the point. "I'm sorry this happened," Jimmy Carter said. "Because this means the bill will be vetoed. There will be no Lock and Dam 26. There will be no waterway user fee."

16

Second Thoughts

In the weeks following the Senate vote, predicting what Jimmy Carter would do about the user-charge bill became one of Washington's favorite guessing games. The vote marked the first time since the "hit list" controversy that Congress had directly challenged the President. Would Carter give in again to the Congressional will (as he had on the hit list), or would he stand firm?

To hear Russell Long tell it, there was nothing to guess about. All through May and June, Long kept assuring everyone that the user-charge/Lock and Dam 26 legislation, as passed by the Senate, would eventually be signed into law. As Long portrayed it, the President's distaste for the bill was mainly a problem of semantics. "He said he wanted a capital-recovery tax," Long observed with a smile shortly after the Senate vote. "And we didn't vote for his capital-recovery tax. That's right. But we passed a tax—sure, it was less than he wanted—and maybe we could just give our tax a new name. We'll call it a 'capital-recovery tax,' and then he can sign this bill." It was not clear—it never was with Long—whether or not this was meant as a joke. In any case, the White House was not amused. Brock Adams continued to insist that the user-charge bill, as passed, was heading for a certain veto. When Carter himself was asked, in a nationally televised press conference, about the prospect for a veto, he gave his questioner an "I'm-glad-you-asked-that" look and responded forcefully. "We asked Congress to impose water-user fees," the President said in determined tones, "to get back part of the cost of the original capital investment. . . . I would veto the Senate-passed bill, yes."

For all the huffing and puffing on both sides, though, the issue did not come to a head—because the waterway bill was delayed by pork-barrel politics.

Both the Stevenson–Domenici and the Long proposals had come up on the Senate floor as amendments to H.R.8309, the House bill Tip O'Neill had put together to avoid a blue slip—the House message that would have killed the bill for good. When the bill had first come over from the House, the Senate Public Works Committee had decided to make it the omnibus vehicle for waterway public-works projects in the 95th Congress. By the time it finally passed the Senate, therefore, H.R.8309 contained not only the user-charge/Lock and Dam 26 package, but another eight dozen amendments authorizing about $2 billion worth of pork-barrel projects.

When O'Neill saw what was happening, he realized that the House would have to get to work on an omnibus bill of its own, so that House members could add any projects they wanted that were not covered in the Senate bill. Once this omnibus bill passed on the House floor, O'Neill would send it to conference together with H.R.8309. Then the conferees could put together a single, final waterway bill containing the user charge, the Alton authorization, and all the other public-works authorizations that members were interested in. To accommodate this plan, O'Neill announced that he would delay appointment of House conferees until the House's own omnibus bill was ready.

The House Public Works Committee held hearings in June, and members filed in by the dozen to make their pleas for some favorite local levee or canal. Since the committee members rarely said no to their colleagues, the list of projects grew rapidly. By the time the committee finished with it, the House bill contained about $2 billion worth of projects, in addition to the $2 billion that had been proposed on the Senate side.

When Jimmy Carter learned from his lobbyists that H.R.8309 might be carrying as much as $4 billion in water projects when it came to the White House, he sent a warning to O'Neill that he would not sign the legislation—even if the contretemps over capital recovery could be resolved. For a President who did not like the pork-barrel game to start with, a $4-billion authorization was just too big to swallow.

This put O'Neill in a difficult position. Several major elements of Carter's legislative program were still pending in Congress, and the President would need to retain all the goodwill he could to get them passed. If Carter were to veto a bill authorizing pork-barrel projects for every state and most Congressional districts, it would stir up so much resentment in Congress that some of the President's most important legislative goals might be threatened. O'Neill was not sure how to avoid this problem altogether, but he did know a way to put off the confrontation. He would just delay a conference on the waterway bill while Congress worked on other legislation. The Speaker, accordingly, simply refused to appoint House conferees. There could be no conference on H.R.8309. Once again, the waterway user charge bill was stopped in its tracks.

As the bright Washington spring turned into a sultry, sweaty Washington summer, the standoff over the waterway bill began to resemble, more and more, a contest between two groups of teenaged hot-rodders racing toward mutual destruction in a game of "chicken." Neither side was willing to veer off an inch to accommodate the other, and, as the Domenici–Carter faction, on one hand, and the Long–barge industry alliance, on the other, both held firmly on course, it appeared increasingly sure that the battle would end up in a murderous head-on collision. If Congress were to send the President a piece of legislation without capital-recovery language and if Carter were to veto it, both sides would lose. The barge interests would lose the authorization for Alton, and Carter would have lost a chance to take credit for a long-delayed change in transportation policy.

As the 95th Congress moved closer to adjournment, the prospects for that collision loomed larger every day. And as the various parties involved in the struggle began to contemplate the impending crash, just about everybody began to have second thoughts.

Pete Domenici, in fact, started having second thoughts within a few hours after he had lost the Senate vote on May 3. "You know," he said the next day, "you could make the argument, you could probably say, that I tried to get too much. If I had just said OK when Russell agreed to a 12-cent tax—if Brock and I had just declared that

a victory and gone home—we could have had us a user-charge bill."
Whatever others might be thinking, Domenici was certain that Carter
would veto a bill that did not contain capital-recovery language. That
meant that Pete Domenici's pet project, the product of two years'
work, the "Domenici Act" that was supposed to be the cornerstone of
his reelection campaign that fall, would not become law. "Yeah, if I
had just taken that tax, even without cost recovery," Domenici said,
talking to himself as much as to his interviewer, "I would have gotten
a bill, and there's not one person in a thousand would know whether
or not it had capital recovery in it."

Brock Adams started getting second thoughts when he heard,
through friends on Capitol Hill, that senior members of the White
House staff were sniping at him behind his back for fouling up the
user-charge business. The Presidential aides were complaining—or
so the Congressional rumor mill had it—that Brock Adams had put
Carter in a box, forcing the President into a major confrontation over
a minor point in a minor bill. The criticism stung—particularly so
because Adams, as a former member of the House, was expected to
be one of the Carter Administration's experts on dealing with Congress. To save the user-charge bill—and his own reputation—Adams
began looking for a way to forge a compromise that would produce a
bill acceptable to everyone.

The barge lobbyists, or most of them, started getting second
thoughts a couple of months after the Senate vote, when it began to
appear that H.R.8309 might never even reach the President's desk. A
few barge-industry lobbyists were pleased when Tip O'Neill had decided not to move forward on H.R.8309; there was still a minority
view in the industry that any waterway tax, no matter how small,
would be a disaster. Those who held this view—Susman, the St.
Louis lawyer, among them—felt that it would be better to get no bill
at all, and thus no water-project authorizations, than to topple the
precedent of toll-free transit. For most of the industry, though, the
idea of no bill at all was intolerable. With no bill, the barge industry
would lose its most important legislative goal, Lock and Dam 26, but
would not really win the user-charge fight—because Domenici, or
Bedell, or somebody would come back in the 96th Congress with
a new user-charge bill. The bargemen, consequently, starting telling
Long and their other Congressional allies that it might be prudent to
find a way to end the impasse.

The railroad lobbyists were telling their friends in Congress the
same thing. Although there was still a Feeney faction within the
industry that wanted to stop Lock and Dam 26 at all costs, most rail

people had come around to the opinion that initiating some water-way user charge, even a small one, was a more important objective. So they, too, were looking for a way to make a deal.

This general shift in attitude was a gradual process, and it would be impossible to pinpoint exactly when the prevailing mood changed. Brayman recalled later, however, when it was that he realized that a resolution might in the offing. "We had heard, starting in June or July," Brayman said, "that Long and his guys wanted to start negotiating seriously again. But, as long as they had Susman doing the talking, we knew we wouldn't get anywhere. Then, one day sometime in the summer, I got a call sort of out of the blue from Bobby Shapiro, and he said, 'Hey, can I get together with you and talk about this waterways [issue]?"

Bernard M. (Bobby) Shapiro, a quiet, 36-year-old lawyer from Virginia, officially carried the title of Chief Counsel to the Joint Committee on Taxation, but unofficially he was known on Capitol Hill as Russell Long's chief negotiator. Long was famous for handling almost all his legislative interests himself, with little reliance on his staff, but he had come to rely on Shapiro for advice and counsel on a broad range of legislation. In the summer of 1978, with the 95th Congress entering its final months, Shapiro was working for Long on such major bills as Carter's energy legislation, a tax-cut bill, the tuition-tax credit, and the Humphrey–Hawkins employment bill. When Shapiro invited himself into negotiations on the waterway fee, then, it was a signal to Brayman that Long might be ready to end the stalemate.

Brayman's first reaction was one of pure suspicion. "Well, naturally, you know, you're going to think something's a little fishy," he explained later. "Here's Russell Long, he's been the A-1 opponent of user fees since we first put in S.790, he's fought us all the way, he's beaten us, effectively, and all of a sudden his guy calls up and offers to negotiate a settlement. So I was thinking, 'Why would Long do that?'"

There was no clear answer, but Brayman decided there could be no harm in talking to Shapiro, and so the two aides began a series of discussions. The two were different people in many ways—Shapiro a reserved, unemotional tactician; Brayman a lively, impassioned politician—but they shared an ability to cut through rhetoric and posturing and get down to the point at hand.

There were two troublesome points that had to be resolved if any kind of waterway-fee bill was to be enacted. The capital-recovery concept was still problematic, because Domenici and the Administration were still interested in creating some linkage between waterway revenues and costs that would serve to limit federal waterway spending, while Long and the water-freight industry were still opposed. The accumulation of pork-barrel projects on H.R.8309 was a problem, too, because the President would not approve a $4-billion authorization bill.

The second problem was resolved first. Rather than try to whittle the $4-billion package down to acceptable size—a process that was sure to alienate the sponsors of any projects cut out of the bill—Brayman and Shapiro decided to jettison it altogether. They would start over with a "clean bill"—a new piece of legislation including only two titles, one authorizing Lock and Dam 26, and one imposing a waterway charge.

But capital recovery was a considerably tougher nut, and the two aides, assisted now and then by lobbyists from the Administration and the various interest groups, spent weeks trying to crack it. Eventually they came up with a solution—acceptable, if not preferable, to both sides—borrowing a concept from federal funding of other transit modes: the trust fund. Brayman agreed that his side would settle for a flat-rate fuel tax of 10 cents per gallon, and Shapiro agreed that his side would permit all the revenues from that tax to be paid into a new "Inland Waterways Trust Fund."

The trust-fund idea was a kind of back-door approach to the goal Domenici had been seeking all along—a limit on the government's waterway expenditures. Legally, it was no limit at all. Shapiro insisted that the legislation should contain specific language stating that waterway expenditures would not be limited to the amount in the trust fund; that is, Congress at any time could spend all the money in the trust fund and still appropriate more money from the Treasury for additional water projects. But Brayman was guessing that, even with such language in the bill, the trust fund would serve, in practice, as a ceiling on waterway expenditures. "If somebody comes up with a big, expensive pork project some year," Brayman explained, "and there's not enough in the trust fund to pay for it, I don't think Congress is going to cough up any money from general revenues. I think they're going to say that project has to wait until there's more bucks in the fund."

Shapiro and Brayman were essentially in agreement by the middle of August, and they quickly won Brock Adams' endorsement of their agreement. But since Congress was in recess then, and Domenici was in New Mexico campaigning for the fall election, it was not until mid-September that Long, Adams, and Domenici were able to get together to discuss the proposal. The three men decided that the "clean-bill idea" and the trust-fund arrangement were the most feasible solutions to their problems, and so they agreed to move ahead with legislation encompassing the Brayman–Shapiro terms. They decided one other point as well: the agreement they had reached would be considered inviolable. Neither side would give in any further to the other.

This last precaution turned out to be a wise one. When Brayman put together a bill along the agreed-on terms, the draft was barely out of the photocopy machine before lobbyists on both sides began complaining about it. The railroads and the environmental groups working with them were unhappy with the trust-fund concept because it did not set an explicit limit on waterway expenditures. The barge lobbyists were livid; they reasoned, just as Brayman had, that the trust fund would act as a de facto limit. But Long and Domenici both told their supporters that nothing could be changed; under the agreement, any adjustment to the plan would kill the whole compromise.

On Friday, October 6, a broad cross section of those who had fought the user-charge wars over the past two years—Senators, Congressmen, Administration officials, railroad executives, barge lobbyists, and staff aides to all of them—met for a final settlement. It was agreed nearly unanimously—only Brent Blackwelder, the chief environmental lobbyists working on the bill, and a few die-hard barge lobbyists refused to go along—that Long and Domenici would introduce a new, "clean" bill authorizing Lock and Dam 26 and imposing a fuel tax that would finance a trust fund for waterway development.

Now there was only one obstacle left—but it was a major obstacle: the calendar.

With every House seat and a third of the Senate up for grabs in the November election, the leadership in both houses was under intense pressure to wrap up the 95th Congress and let members go home to campaign. Byrd, in the Senate, and O'Neill, in the House, had originally promised adjournment by mid-September. When the backlog of unfinished legislation made that impossible, the date slipped to October 1—prompting howls of outrage from members facing tough reelection challenges. When that deadline, too, became impossible to meet, Byrd and O'Neill extended the adjournment date two more weeks, to October 14, with absolute assurance that there would be no further extensions. Any bills unfinished by then, O'Neill said, "will be left to die—which is probably what a lot of them deserve anyway."

When the waterway user charge agreement was reached, then, there were precisely eight days remaining in the 95th Congress. Since the agreement centered on the introduction of a clean bill—a bill that would have to start at ground zero and work its way through both houses, a conference, and final passage—it seemed impossible that the compromise plan could be enacted in the 95th Congress. The whole legislative process, with its emphasis on detailed consideration and extended deliberation, was designed to prevent eight-day wonders from becoming law.

There were only three men in the 95th Congress who had enough skill at manipulating the rules of procedure (and enough authority to get away with it) to move the waterway user charge bill from introduction to enactment in eight days. The Senate Majority Leader could have done it; the House Speaker could have done it. But both Byrd and O'Neill were too wrapped up in other problems to worry about passing a waterway bill in the final week of Congress. There was only one other person who could achieve that legislative miracle: Russell Billiu Long.

17

Good Old Boy

The Constitution of the United States declares quite clearly (Article I, Section 3) that "No Person shall be a Senator who shall not have attained the Age of thirty Years," but this formality did not stop the people of Louisiana, on November 2, 1948, from electing a 29-year-old lawyer and Navy veteran to a seat in the U.S. Senate. The Senator-elect, Russell Billiu Long, celebrated his thirtieth birthday before he was formally sworn in the following January, making the whole business legal, albeit unusual. But then, just about every political achievement of Louisiana Democrats bearing the name Long has been unusual, because the Longs of Louisiana built a dynasty that has had no match in twentieth-century American politics. When Russell Long won his Senate seat, he became not only the youngest U.S. Senator but also the only person ever to succeed both his father and his mother in that body. During his first term as Louisiana's junior Senator, Russell's uncle Earl was Louisiana's governor, his aunt Blanche was Louisiana's Democratic National Committeewoman, and his uncle George served in Congress from Louisiana's 8th District. (Two other Longs, Russell's cousins Gillis and Speedy, represented the 8th District after George's death.)

The progenitor of this prodigious political clan was Russell's father, Huey P. Long, the zestful, clownish, larger-than-life populist who was, depending on which history book you read, either a savior of the downtrodden or a dictator who imposed one-man rule on an entire state. During his 18 years in public life, Huey transformed Louisiana from a state run by Standard Oil and other large firms to a state run by a single large family—the Longs. After his election to the U.S. Senate, in 1932, Huey Long began to work his political magic on a national constituency, and there was wide speculation that he might unseat President Roosevelt in 1936. That speculation became academic on the night of September 8, 1935, when a young doctor who had a grievance against the Longs swept past Huey's armed bodyguards and murdered him with a single bullet through the navel.

One hundred fifty thousand Louisianans poured into Baton Rouge for the funeral; the state constitution was amended to make Huey Long's birthday a legal holiday; the mourning went on for months. For at least one person, it never really ended. Twenty-eight years later, when the members of the U.S. Senate stood up one by one to offer their condolences to the widow and children of John F. Kennedy, most observers agreed that Russell Long, who was not generally known for moving oratory, gave the most poignant speech of all. "How well I know that special grief," Long said sadly.

The martyrdom of Huey Long guaranteed the political success of the dynasty. Huey's widow, Rose, immediately took his seat in the Senate. His brother Earl became governor. As the fallen hero's eldest son, Russell Long effectively acquired a safe seat in the U.S. Senate while he was still an undergraduate at Louisiana State. In 1948, when he came within striking distance of the legal age, he ran away with the balloting for the Senate, and he did so again in every election thereafter.

Even after five terms in the Senate, though, Russell Long hardly looked the part of a powerful force in the federal establishment. A likable, good-old-boy type with a paunch, a shuffle, and a puffy face marked by a nose that looked like a half-inflated red balloon, he seemed more like the kind of person you'd find astride a fence rail along some country road than behind a desk on the floor of the U.S. Senate. He talked like a country boy, too. Running on in the singsong voice that cracked on the high notes when he was excited, he never seemed to be able to correct all the "You ain't's" and the "He don't's" that slipped into his discourse.

But that was all part of the act. Despite appearances, Russell Long worked his way up in the Senate on the strength of a wily political intelligence, a quick legal mind, and a textbook familiarity with the rules of procedure. He developed into one of Washington's leading policy experts in such fields as Social Security, energy, and welfare. From his seat on the Finance Committee, he became an acknowledged master of one of the most pervasive but arcane fields of legislation: the federal tax code.

After his ascendancy to the chairmanship of Finance, in 1966, Long became one of the Senate's leading power brokers as well. Almost every Senator, at one time or another, wanted to pass a tax break for some constituent, and Long was almost always willing to accommodate. The price for the chairman's cooperation was sometimes stated plainly, and sometimes left unsaid, but he always exacted a price— in the form of a vote for some bill that Russell Long wanted passed. He was, moreover, an equal-opportunity horse trader; Long would give to, and get from, Democrats and Republicans, liberals and conservatives. For a decade, his strongest opponent on the Finance Committee was Walter Mondale, the liberal Minnesotan who complained angrily about the "special-interest tax loopholes" that Long was always steering through the committee. But when Mondale introduced a tax provision designed to help Investors' Diversified Services, Inc., a big Minneapolis investment firm whose executives had helped bankroll Mondale's political career, Long resisted the temptation to punish an adversary. He supported Mondale's bill, and defended it when the press criticized Mondale for hypocrisy. After that, Mondale was not quite so forceful in his opposition to Russell Long.

By the beginning of the 95th Congress, when Pete Domenici introduced his waterway bill, Russell Long's ability to get his way in the Senate was almost legendary. He didn't win all the time—no Senator could—but he seemed to win more often than almost anybody else. That was why Domenici took pains to keep his bill away from Long's committee, and that was why it was so surprising when Domenici passed S.790 in a head-to-head tilt with Long. Long, of course, prevailed on the capital-recovery point in the second Senate vote, in 1978, but, as he noted afterward, Domenici was the real winner. "If Russell Long had gotten his way," Long said the day after the second vote, "there wouldn't be any waterway tax at all."

Long, in fact, had developed a genuine admiration for his New Mexican adversary during the struggle over the user charge. Domenici had won by using the same tools that Russell Long liked to rely on—adroit parliamentary maneuvering, intense person-to-person lobbying, and sheer political power (Presidential power, in this case, since Domenici did not have much of his own). As a result, Long began to feel that Domenici deserved to get some kind of user-charge legislation out of the 95th Congress. "I hope we get a bill," Long said in mid-summer of 1978. "And I hope everybody calls it the 'Domenici Bill.'" Thus when the stalemate over capital recovery threatened, in the last weeks of the 95th Congress, to kill all hope for passage of a waterway bill, Russell Long personally intervened, telling Shapiro to get busy and come up with a solution.

There was another factor, too, in Long's gradual decision to help Domenici enact a user-charge bill. Despite his geographic ties to the water-freight industry, the Senator from Louisiana had become increasingly disenchanted with the barge lines and their Washington lobbyists as the legislative battle wore on. As Long saw it, the original Senate vote on S.790 was largely due to a strategic blunder by the barge lobby. Long, after all, had been prepared to filibuster on the bill, but the barge lobbyists had stopped him by saying they had the votes to win. And then, having lost the first round, the lobbyists had refused to face up to that fact. Russell Long had been at first amused, then annoyed, and finally downright angry to hear barge lobbyists still talking about defeating the user charge altogether, even after both House and Senate had approved the concept. Long grew angrier still when the barge lines placed their trust in Susman, the unyielding negotiator whose basic tactic was intransigence. Gradually, the meetings between Long and the barge industry turned into furious shouting matches, and the Senator effectively gave up on his erstwhile allies.

It was Adlai Stevenson, though, who finally cemented Long's determination to help Domenici pass a bill. Stevenson, like almost everyone else, had been dismayed to see the stalemate develop over H.R.8309, and he eventually concluded that no user-charge bill was going to pass in the 95th Congress. Since his primary goal had always been passage of a Lock and Dam 26 authorization, Stevenson decided, in the last weeks of Congress, to try once more to enact the Alton authorization without any user charge.

By September of 1978, the Senate was in session six days a week to move through its mountain of unfinished business. One Saturday afternoon, when the floor was almost deserted, Stevenson introduced, as an amendment to the pending legislation, a new bill authorizing the lock and dam. Senator Ted Stevens, an Alaska Republican who was present to protect the interests of absent GOP members, strolled over to ask Stevenson what this was all about. The Senator from Illinois replied that this was just a simple water project, completely harmless; in fact, Stevenson went on, his amendment was "virtually identical" to a bill that had passed the Senate before, so no Republican would mind if it went through again. With that assurance, Stevens let the amendment come up and then walked off the floor. A few minutes later, the Senate had passed, by voice vote, a bill it had rejected twice before: a Lock and Dam 26 authorization with no user charge at all.

Hal Brayman was halfway through his morning doughnut the following Monday when he discovered this ploy. "I was just skimming through the goddamn *Record*," Brayman recalled later, "to find out what had happened Saturday, and all of a sudden I went through the goddamn roof!" Stevenson's coup, Brayman knew, might be fatal. If enough members decided that this Stevenson amendment might get through the House and be signed into law after all, there would be insufficient support for the Brayman–Shapiro compromise package, which was then nearly complete. Brayman and Rawls put in a panicky call to Domenici, who was in a remote corner of New Mexico pursuing a tight campaign schedule. "We're going to get screwed on this thing!" Rawls told the Senator in tones of desperation, "We'd had it all worked out, and now Adlai's screwed it all up!" Domenici headed back to Albuquerque to catch the midnight flight to Washington.

At 7:00 the next morning, when Domenici, gaunt, unshaven, and red-eyed from his sleepless night in transit, arrived at the Senate Office Building, he was met by Rawls and Brayman, and the three stepped into an elevator to ride to Domenici's office on the fourth floor. There was one other person in the elevator: Russell Long. "Good God, Pete, you look terrible," Long said solicitously. "You been up all night? Just come in from New Mexico? Gee, I hope you didn't fly back here just because of this waterway business. There's no problem—I'm going to take care of that for you."

Long explained that he had been shocked by Stevenson's Saturday afternoon ploy. The Senate could only operate, he said, if Senators could rely on each other's word. Stevenson, by concealing the real effect of his floor amendment, had broken that unwritten rule. And Russell Long was not about to let Adlai Stevenson, or anyone else, get away with that kind of skullduggery.

"You don't have to worry, Pete," Long said as he stepped off the elevator. "As soon as we settle up for good on the terms of this thing, we're going to pass you a bill."

18

Bingo!

The task facing Russell Long, as he set out, in the final days of the 95th Congress, to win passage of the new waterway package—authorizing Lock and Dam 26 and establishing an Inland Waterways Trust Fund to be financed by a fuel tax on commercial barges—was a formidable one.

The second session of the 95th Congress had been one of the most fractious sessions in recent history. Disputes between Republicans and Democrats, between junior and senior members, and between the Congressional leadership and the White House had so delayed things that, with a week to go before adjournment, about two dozen major bills and scores of minor ones were still awaiting final action. Long would have to steer the waterway package through Congress during one of its busiest weeks ever. Moreover, Long would have to start his waterway-tax bill in the Senate—raising once again the risk of a Constitutional challenge, under the origination clause, when the legislation went to the House.

But Russell Long was equal to this challenge. Over the years he had seen numerous pieces of controversial tax legislation come down to the wire under similar circumstances, and he had become a master of the Congressional endgame. Thus, while all the other principals in the user-charge drama were biting their nails and fretting that the compromise bill could not possibly be enacted before adjournment, Long was strolling the Capitol corridors with the serene smile of a riverboat gambler who has a stock of aces up his sleeve.

Long's hidden aces in this legislative showdown were a group of minor tax bills that the House had passed and sent to the Senate earlier in the session. In every Congress, such bills—each making some obscure change in some obscure section of the Internal Revenue Code—would come over to the Senate and be referred to the Finance Committee. Each year Long would hold a few of them in limbo, without scheduling hearings or a mark-up session. Then, when he needed a vehicle for some last-minute legislative initiative, he would pull out one of the minor House bills and send it directly to the Senate floor, where the last-minute legislation could be passed as a floor amendment to the House-passed bill. The whole package— House bill and Senate rider—could then go directly to a House–Senate conference. This procedure, which Long had perfected over the years, permitted him to get the bill through the Senate and into conference in whirlwind fashion. Further, since the vehicle he used was always a revenue bill that had originated in the House, Long could send Senate legislation forward in this manner without risking a blue slip under the origination clause.

Long explained this system in the meeting on October 6, when the principals in the user-charge negotiations had worked out a final agreement for a "clean" bill encompassing the Brayman–Shapiro plan. Brayman was duly impressed by the scheme of legislative legerdemain that Long set forth, but he was not convinced it would work. "Senator," he said skeptically, "can this bill be passed in a week?"

"Oh, sure," Long said calmly. "We just have to find a vehicle, and that's no problem. I've always got a few little bills back in the office."

Long went back to the office a few days later and came up with H.R.8533, a House-passed measure that bore the title "A bill to amend the Internal Revenue Code of 1954 to provide that income from the conducting of certain bingo games by certain tax-exempt organizations will not be subject to tax." It was a textbook case of special-interest tax legislation. The bill—which declared that the profits earned by "political organizations" on bingo games would not be subject to federal income tax—was written in general terms and had general application, but in fact it had been introduced with a single beneficiary in mind. The sponsor, Representative William M. Brodhead, a Democrat from Michigan, was interested in saving some money for Michigan's Democratic Party, which traditionally held bingo games to raise campaign money, and which did not want to pay income tax on its bingo earnings. When Brodhead had drafted his bill, however, he had astutely written it so that the tax exemption applied not only to political parties but also to charitable and fraternal groups that used bingo to raise funds. Since no member of Congress was happy voting against a tax break for charities and fraternal organizations, the Brodhead bill had passed the House with ease.

Even with a House-passed revenue bill as his vehicle, however, Long still had some problems to overcome in winning passage of the waterway legislation. His high-speed plan for the bill violated Senate rules left and right—rules governing how a bill should move from committee to the floor, rules setting certain minimum time periods before a bill could come up for a final floor vote. But the rules also set forth the means for getting around the rules—through a procedure called "unanimous consent." Whenever a Senator can get all the other Senators on the floor to agree to something—to consent unanimously—the rules can be waived. Unanimous consent is used dozens of times every day to keep the Senate moving along; Long would use the same process to circumvent the rules and bring the bingo tax bill, with its waterway rider, to the floor.

The first time Long tried that, though—on the evening of October 9, five days before the end of the Congress—something went wrong. When Long stood up to offer a routine unanimous-consent request "to discharge the Finance Committee from further consideration . . . of H.R.8533," Senator William Proxmire, the Wisconsin Democrat, promptly objected. Proxmire, a staunch supporter of the waterway fee, had decided that the 10-cent fuel tax and the trust-fund concept were not good enough; he thought no bill at all would be better than the trust-fund measure now being offered. Since a single objection was enough to sidetrack Long's plan, Proxmire had effectively stopped the user-charge bill from proceeding along the only course it had left.

After the Senate had finished work for the day, proponents of the compromise plan began an all-out effort to convince Proxmire to change his mind. Long and Gaylord A. Nelson, Proxmire's Democratic colleague from Wisconsin, worked on the Senator himself, while Brayman ran through the whole tortured history of the bill for Howard Shuman, Proxmire's top staff aide. Proxmire was finally persuaded that the trust-fund bill represented the only user-charge legislation that could possibly pass the 95th Congress, and the Senator agreed, reluctantly, to go along.

The next day Long rose again on the Senate floor and asked unanimous consent to have H.R.8533 discharged from committee and brought up immediately on the floor. This time nobody objected. It was the third time the waterway user charge had come up in the Senate, and now it was coming up without Pete Domenici, who was back in New Mexico on the campaign trail. Domenici's Republican colleague from New Mexico, Harrison (Jack) Schmitt, was on the floor, with Rawls and Brayman at his side, to be on guard against unexpected developments, but that precaution turned out to be unnecessary. By now, there was no one left to oppose the bill. After 40 minutes of lackadaisical debate, the amendment to the bingo tax bill was passed by voice vote.

As Long had planned things, H.R.8533 should next have gone to a conference committee, where the House conferees were to agree to the Senate amendment containing the waterway package. But in the rush to adjournment, that turned out to be unworkable. Members of the tax-writing committees in both houses were already tied up in all-day conferences on two other major tax bills. Ullman, the chairman of House Ways and Means, flatly refused to let Long convene a third conference. Long, accordingly, had to revise his scenario slightly. Instead of going to conference, the bingo bill would go back to the House. If the House would pass a user-charge/Lock and Dam 26 amendment identical to the one the Senate had adopted, no conference would be necessary.

Because Long, Domenici, and Adams had been careful to include Ullman and O'Neill in their planning sessions while the final compromise was being developed and because most elements of the railroad and barge industries were backing the compromise, it was not difficult to arrange a House floor vote on the bingo bill and its new Senate rider. O'Neill decided to bring the measure to the floor under a short-cut procedure called "suspension," in which the normal rules are suspended and legislation can come to the floor without having received a "ticket" from the Rules Committee. He scheduled the bill for an hour of debate and a final vote on October 11, the day after it passed the Senate.

It would have been totally out of character, though, for the waterway bill to reach the end of its circuitous path to passage without some last-minute obstacle cropping up, and sure enough, just a few minutes before the package was due to come up on the House floor, a new problem emerged. An aide to Brodhead, the Michigan Democrat who had introduced the original bingo tax bill, skimmed through the

Senate legislation and discovered a major flaw: the Senate had made
the waterway package a substitute for the bingo provision, rather
than an addition ot it. As a result, the Senate's "bingo bill" included
the waterway compromise, all right, but not the bingo tax exemption.
Brodhead and Bob Traxler, another Michigan Democrat, immediately protested to O'Neill.

The Speaker was sympathetic, but he was also in a bind. Since
there was no time to arrange a conference on the waterway legislation, the House and Senate had to pass identical versions of the bill;
if the House were now to add back the bingo tax language, the two
versions would no longer be identical, and thus nothing—neither
the bingo exemption nor the waterway compromise—would be
enacted. On the other hand, O'Neill could not stand by idly when the
Senate had killed a bill that had passed the House. So the Speaker
took the bill off the House calendar and called Long to find out what
was up.

O'Neill never did discover whether or not Long had purposely left
out the bingo provision (to this day, Long will not explain what
happened). But after three days of discussions, a new plan was
agreed to. The House would pass H.R.8533 in the form the Senate
had approved it. Then both houses would pass concurrent resolu-
tions putting the bingo tax exemption back into the bill. If no more
problems came up, the end result would be a bingo/waterway package approved in identical form by both houses—and thus ready to be
sent to the White House.

On the afternoon of Friday, the thirteenth of October—26 hours
before the 95th Congress was scheduled to adjourn—the waterway
user charge came before the House of Representatives for the last
time. The brief debate was marked by a pervasive aura of anticlimax;
all the wars had been fought, all the deals had been struck, and
everybody knew that the waterway bill was finally going to pass. The
speeches, accordingly, were predictable and perfunctory—except for
one electric moment. "The gentleman from Iowa, Mr. Bedell, is recognized for four minutes," the presiding officer said, and suddenly
there was Berkley Bedell at the front of the chamber, still arguing
with all his force for a direct link between the government's expenditures and the users' tax. "I urge you to vote down H.R.8533," Bedell
said, his voice a blend of sorrow and anger, "so we can obtain a user
fee that will transform the users themselves into watchdogs to moni-
tor every [water] project's cost-effectiveness."

Bedell's last-minute appeal was not quite as hopeless as it
appeared. There was no question that most House members were

ready to vote for the bingo/waterway package legislation, if for no other reason that just to get this pesky issue out of the way once and for all. But passage of the bill would take more than a simple majority of the House; under the shortcut suspension procedure, a bill requires the approval of two-thirds of the members present. When O'Neill called for a roll-call vote on the measure, it looked for several minutes as if Bedell and other critics of the compromise legislation might get just enough allies to keep the majority supporting the bill under the two-thirds margin. Then, in the last few minutes of the roll call, the "aye" votes crept up beyond the two-thirds point, and when the Speaker pounded his gavel and announced that "all time has expired," the vote stood at 287 to 123 in favor of H.R.8533—13 votes more than the minimum needed for passage. On the penultimate day of the 95th Congress—one year, seven months, three weeks, and a day after it had been introduced—the waterway user charge bill had become a waterway user charge act.

19

Golden Opportunity

Within minutes after House passage of the user-charge legislation, the Carter Administration's public relations apparatus swung into action to make sure that the President received due credit for his role in enacting this historic change in federal transportation policy. Brock Adams' press secretary began calling reporters less than half an hour after the bill had passed to spread the word that "Congress today adopted another element of President Carter's national transportation program." Later that afternoon, a White House press aide described the House vote as "a major victory for the President." Neither Adams' office nor the White House made any mention of Pete Domenici, Berkley Bedell, Russell Long, or any other members of Congress who had been involved in the long legislative struggle.

The President's advisers, however, felt that the waterway bill could be used for much more than a self-congratulatory press release. Gerald Rafshoon, an advertising executive whom Carter had hired to help the Administration create a forceful public image, urged the President to hold a gala public ceremony, preferably someplace outside of Washington, for the signing of the measure. As Rafshoon and other political advisers saw it, the waterway bill was a perfect symbol of a President standing up for the taxpayers' interests—and forcing a reluctant Congress to go along. To sign the bill into law in some brief private moment in the Oval Office would be to waste a golden opportunity.

When word spread through the White House that Rafshoon was looking for a public occasion somewhere in the country for the signing of the user-charge/Lock and Dam 26 legislation, Vice President Mondale immediately came up with a suggestion: the bill should be signed, Mondale said, at a big Democratic political rally in Minneapolis. Minneapolis, after all, was a major barge port—the point of origin or destination for much of the traffic moving through the Alton lock. And the Minnesota Democrats were in serious trouble going into the November election—badly in need of the kind of political tonic that a Presidential visit can provide.

That the Minnesota Democratic Party could be in trouble was startling in itself. Since the late 1940s, when a political tyro named Hubert Horatio Humphrey had forged an alliance of urban liberals, farmers, and union members, the state party (formally known as the Democratic-Farmer-Labor Party, or DFL) had been one of the strongest political organizations anywhere. The DFL had provided the nation two vice presidents, Humphrey and Mondale, and by the middle 1970s it controlled both houses of the state legislature, most of the state's seats in the House, both Senate seats, and the governorship. But then things went sour. In January 1977, when Mondale left the Senate to be sworn in as Vice President, Governor Wendell Anderson had appointed himself to Mondale's Senate seat, and the Lieutenant Governor Rudy Perpich had moved up to the governorship. In January 1978, when Hubert Humphrey died of cancer, his Senate seat went, by appointment, to his widow, Muriel. All of a sudden the DFL's top three officeholders were all holding offices they had not been elected to—and the voters, according to opinion polls, were furious. In the election campaign that fall, polls showed that Anderson, who was seeking election to the Senate seat he had given himself, and Perpich, who was seeking election to the governorship he had inherited, were both running neck-and-neck with their Republican challengers, and the GOP candidate was leading in the special election to fill Humphrey's Senate seat. Throughout the summer and fall of 1978, therefore, Mondale had been looking for a way to get Carter to Minnesota so he could stump for the Democratic candidates and help the party raise campaign money. Now, Mondale figured, there was a perfect reason for the trip. To sign the waterway bill anyplace other than Minneapolis would be to waste a golden opportunity.

There was a fundamental logical flaw, however, in the Mondale plan. Why should the President choose a Democratic rally in Minnesota as the place to sign a bill that had been uniformly opposed by

Minnesota's Democrats? Although the Minnesotans in Congress had backed the Lock and Dam 26 authorization, they had fought hard against the effort to link a user-charge provision to the authorization bill. Anderson had voted against the Domenici–Carter position every time it came up. Muriel Humphrey, after giving Carter what he thought was a commitment of support, had voted against him on the floor. James L. Oberstar, a DFL Congressman from the "iron range" country around Duluth, had been one of the most forceful opponents of the user charge in the House. Of all the Minnesota Congressmen, in fact, only one, Albert H. Quie, had actively supported the user-charge legislation. But since Quie was a Republican, and was the GOP nominee challenging Perpich for the governorship, Carter could hardly praise his work on the bill at a DFL political rally.

If anyone at the White House raised this logical objection, however, the objection was overruled. At 7:10 on the evening of Saturday, October 21—eight days after the final Congressional vote on the waterway bill—Jimmy Carter, accompanied by Walter Mondale, Brock Adams, and the enormous retinue of assistants, security men, reporters, and photographers who swarm around a President wherever he goes, swept into a meeting room at the Minneapolis auditorium. After greeting the various DFL dignitaries waiting there for him—Wendell Anderson, Muriel Humphrey, and James Oberstar among them—Carter stepped to the podium and got down to the business at hand.

The President first explained in some detail the importance of Lock and Dam 26, to the nation in general and to Minnesota in particular. He then discussed the long fight in Congress to pass the authorization bill. "I wanted to come here," Carter said, "where you are so heavily interested in this project to put my signature on the bill, which will make it law." There was another section of the law, of course, and Carter explained that in a curious way, making the user-charge legislation sound like some long-sought boon to the barge industry that the barge lobbyists had been fighting tooth and nail to win. "Ever since Franklin Roosevelt was President," he said, "there has been an attempt made to let those who use our waterways contribute to the improvement and construction of projects that would enhance the use of the waterways, waterway user fees. This bill authorizes that to be done."

Things got even more curious when Carter when on to explain who should get the credit for getting the bill passed. "I would particularly like to thank the Minnesota Congressional delegation," the President said, turning to nod to the Minnesotans just behind him.

"Senator Wendell Anderson . . . is very helpful in passing legislation important to your state, as you can well see. And of course, Senator Humphrey, both Hubert and his wife, Muriel, have been of great help in getting this bill passed. The members of the House have done the same.

"Also," the President went on, "since we are signing this bill outside Washington, I think it is good to recognize, for the media itself, some others who have worked very hard on this legislation." Carter then proceeded to name a group of Democrats who had been "instrumental" in helping pass the user-charge/lock and dam legislation; he singled out Senators Stevenson, Long, and Randolph, and Congressmen Ullman and Johnson. About midway through this recital, the President suddenly seemed to remember one other person who might deserve mention. He paused for the briefest moment—and then mentioned the name. "And Senator Domenici," the President said quickly.

Since the President was speaking as politician rather than as political scientist, it was not particularly surprising that he should give a partisan twist to his description of the waterway bill and its path through Congress. If he had really wanted to explain why this hardy legislative perennial had finally blossomed, however, Carter would have had to discuss the interplay of four factors that determine the fate of every bill introduced in every Congress: policy, personality, parliamentary procedure, and politics.

It would be naive to suggest that any proposed legislation that is generally perceived in Congress to enhance some desirable public-policy objective will be enacted into law, or that any bill generally believed to encompass an undesirable policy will be defeated. Every member of Congress, or at least every honest one, will admit that on occasion, because of political pressures, he has voted for some bills he disagreed with and against some he personally favored. Still, the force of a good idea is a powerful influence. From the beginning of his uphill fight to pass the waterway bill, Pete Domenici benefited from the general perception, at least among those members not closely allied with the barge industry, that it was a good idea to end the barge lines' free ride.

Rawls and Brayman found this particularly true on the staff level; they repeatedly found that Senate aides, who were generally more isolated from political pressure than their bosses, were willing and even anxious to lobby their Senators on behalf of the user charge.

Among Senators themselves, the feeling that—as Senator Edward M. (Teddy) Kennedy, the Massachusetts Democrat, put it before the first Senate vote—"Pete Domenici is on to a pretty sensible idea" helped win the votes of a whole squadron of other liberal Democrats: Gary Hart, of Colorado; Birch Bayh, of Indiana; and Howard M. Metzenbaum, of Ohio—who would normally have nothing to do with one of Pete Domenici's proposals.

The publicity the bill received helped spread this "good-policy notion." "You know," Domenici said in a postmortem after his bill had finally been enacted, "there's probably 500 good-policy ideas floating around on the Hill at any one time, but most of them just aren't getting on the front page of the *Post* every week." The *Washington Post's* continuing coverage of the legislation, together with the dozens of newspapers around the country that endorsed the user charge on their editorial pages, gave Domenici's idea a degree of visibility it could not otherwise have achieved—and strengthened the perception in Congress that the bill made sense.

But the user-charge legislation was no more sensible in 1978 than it had been in 1938 and all the years thereafter when it had fallen by the wayside almost immediately after it was introduced. Policy considerations alone had never been enough to pass the waterway bill, and policy alone would not have done the job in the 95th Congress, either. In the 95th, though, this "good-policy initiative" got a strong push from personal factors—from the personal chemistry among the various people who got involved with the bill on its long road from introduction to enactment.

Pete Domenici's tenacious determination to keep at it despite countless setbacks, Russell Long's wily skill at getting things done, Jimmy Carter's stubborn insistence on getting involved in an area that most Presidents leave to Congress—all these personal traits were major assets for the waterway bill. Domenici's personal popularity was also a significant factor. Henry Bellmon, the Oklahoma Republican, to cite one example, should have been a sure vote against the user charge: the barge business was growing rapidly in his state, and the chairman of his chief committee was dead set against the bill. Set against these considerations was one countervailing point: Pete Domenici was Henry Bellmon's closest Senate friend. On the crucial vote, Bellmon voted with his friend. Russell Long, too, was influenced by personal considerations. Although it is always difficult to discern precisely what motivates the enigmatic Senator from Louisiana, it seems safe to say that Long's shift from adamant opposition to active support stemmed at least partly from his personal admiration for Domenici's skill and hard work—from the feeling, as Long himself put it late in 1978, that "Senator Domenici *deserves* to get a bill."

Similarly, the personal friendship between Pete Domenici and Brock Adams was one of the factors that prompted the Democratic Administration to undertake an intense effort to pass a Republican's bill. And it was Adams' friendship with O'Neill, in turn, that prompted the Speaker to solve the blue-slip dilemma. Without these friendships, there would have been no user charge.

Nor would the user charge have been enacted without the labyrinthine procedural manipulations that Domenici, O'Neill, and finally Long engaged in to move the bill around the various obstacles in its path to passage. The legislation strayed repeatedly from the standard bill-becomes-a-law flowchart set forth in the high school civics books—but then, most legislation does. There are some bills in each Congress that proceed neatly along the prescribed path— subcommittee to full committee to Rules Committee (in the House) to floor vote to conference committee to floor vote to President's signature. Most, though, take an uncharted turn or two along the way. Almost every sponsor tries, as the proponents of the user charge did, to steer his or her bill along the path of least resistance. If Domenici had not done that, the waterway user charge legislation would still be moldering today near the bottom of the Senate Finance Committee's "pending-business" roster.

But, while the bill's procedural twists and turns were not particularly unusual, the measure's political pedigree was definitely out of the ordinary. Congress is, of course, an intensely political place, a place where personal and party politics influence everything that happens. But it would take a long search to find another instance where a conservative Republican Senator's pet project was pushed through to passage by the active intervention of a Democratic President. The symbiotic relationship that developed between Republican Domenici and Democrat Carter on the waterway bill was essential to its success. Without the President, Domenici could not have made his hostage strategy hold up on the Senate floor. And, without Domenici, the Administration would probably not have been assured of the Republican votes it needed to make the veto threat stick.

This ad hoc alliance grew out of the quite distinct personal goals of three politicans. A major reason for Pete Domenici's zeal to pass a user-charge bill was his desire to show his constituents (and his Senate colleagues) that he was an effective Senator. Brock Adams had

a similar interest in the bill: Winning this difficult legislative struggle would demonstrate to his employer in the White House and to
people he worked with all over official Washington that the new
Secretary of Transportation was a man who could get things done.
Jimmy Carter's decision to back the measure with the full force of
his office stemmed partly from his personal distaste for the waterway
pork barrel and partly from his ambition to take credit for an achievement that had eluded seven of his predecessors. It was politics, in
short, that made these men into a team working for the waterway bill.

And it was politics, of course, that brought the President to the
rally in Minneapolis for the last action needed to make the legislation
a public law. At the end of his speech, after one last word of thanks to
the Minnesota Congressional delegation, Carter showed the audience
an ornately printed document bearing the final text of the bill as both
houses had passed it. "Now I will sign into law House Bill 8533," the
President said, and he bent over and scrawled "Jimmy Carter" in
quick, bold strokes. Someone in the audience started clapping, and
the applause spread in ragged fashion through the audience and up
to the platform, where Mondale, Anderson, Humphrey, and Oberstar joined in with minimal enthusiasm. And thus it was that, to the
polite applause of its erstwhile opponents, the waterway user charge
became the law of the land.

Epilogue

The President's political foray to Minneapolis turned out to be far less successful than Rafshoon and Mondale had hoped. The Minnesota Democrats were split by a bitter factional dispute that fall, and Carter was unlucky enough to get trapped in no-man's-land between the two sides. When he stepped onto the platform at the DFL rally, he shook hands with the leader of one of the factions, a courtesy that drew a resounding chorus of boos and catcalls from thousands of members of the opposing faction in the audience. The picture of a Democratic President being jeered at a big Democratic rally was irresistible to the press, and the booing incident was the major topic in the next morning's news stories about the rally. The bill-signing that Rafshoon had worked so hard to arrange received passing mention in some newspapers, none in most. And if the Presidential visit was a tonic for the DFL, as Mondale had expected it to be, the tonic wasn't potent enough; in the election two weeks later, the Minnesota Republicans swept the governorship and both Senate seats.

Two thousand miles to the southwest, however, the waterway bill had a much more propitious impact on Pete Domenici's race for reelection. The word went out among railroad executives all over the country that the Senator from New Mexico deserved a favor, and they responded by contributing more than $30,000 to his campaign treasury. (A group of barge executives, led by Harry Cook, tried to stir

133

up contributions for Domenici's Democratic challenger, Toney Anaya, but Anaya received only a few thousand dollars from the bargemen.) More important, the success of the legislation gave Domenici, just as he had hoped, the aura of a successful legislator. Most of New Mexico's newspapers endorsed his reelection, and in most cases the endorsements cited the waterway bill as proof of his legislative skill. Domenici won a second Senate term by a comfortable margin.

The waterway bill played a smaller role in Charles Percy's reelection campaign in Illinois, although Percy rode in a "Victory Parade" down the main street of Alton, Illinois, after the bill was passed and told the local newspaper that he was pleased to have contributed to the success of the legislation. Percy won reelection in a tight race. Another Senator who squeaked by on Election Day was Jennings Randolph. The West Virginian won reelection with 50.1 percent of the vote after Jimmy Carter made three separate trips to campaign for him. Howard Baker won by a landslide in Tennessee, despite Democratic criticism of his vote for the user charge when S.790 was before the Senate. In northwestern Iowa, Berkley Bedell was easily reelected to the House, as were all the other House members who had been involved in the waterway bill's odyssey.

Back in Washington, the lobbyists collected their fees and moved on to new issues. In April 1979, though, just about everybody who had lobbied either for or against the user-charge legislation got together for a sort of reunion in a sprawling executive suite just down the hall from Brock Adams' office on the top floor of the Transportation Department's headquarters. The occasion was a party in honor of Sue Williams, who had finally been promoted to the office, title, and salary she should have received when she had first come to work at the Department. "I think there was some prejudice against a woman in this job when Sue got here," Adams said over a cup of fruit punch. "But she earned this promotion by getting that waterway toll passed."

Adams himself did not fare as well. Contrary to his expectation, passage of the waterway bill did little to ameliorate relations between the Secretary and the White House staff. If anything, in fact, the bill made things worse, because Hamilton Jordan, Carter's chief of staff, complained that Adams had unfairly hogged the credit for the user-charge success story. In August 1979, during a turbulent week when Carter cashiered four cabinet members, Adams was called to the White House and given specific conditions to abide by to stay on the job. Most of official Washington expected Adams, a good team player, to go along. Instead, he emerged from his meeting with the President in a defiant mood and actually started listing conditions that he thought Jimmy Carter should abide by. For this impertinence, Adams was fired the next day—and it was generally agreed that his gutsy departure was the high point of his cabinet term. He went on to practice law in the Washington, D.C., office of a Seattle firm.

Joe Feeney's "laundry" went out of business. After the details were reported in the press, the environmental groups decided that they could no longer take railroad money under any guise. But Feeney continued his battle against Lock and Dam 26; having lost in Congress, he carried on with his fight in the courts, and a federal judge agreed to hold a trial on Feeney's contention that the Corps of Engineers had failed to comply with federal environmental laws in planning the project. The Corps went ahead with planning and design work for the Alton project while the case was pending. It would be years, though, before the legal questions could all be settled.

The judge's decision had no effect on the waterway user charge, and the new tax entered the statute books. When the 1979 edition of the Internal Revenue Code went to press, it included a brand-new section, Section 4042, declaring: "There is hereby imposed a tax on any liquid used during any calendar quarter by any person as a fuel in a vessel in commercial waterway transportation. . . . The amendments made by this section shall take effect on October 1, 1980."

On January 15, 1979, the 96th Congress formally convened, and the opening session was marked by the usual flood of the usual perennial bills. There was a marigold bill, and a renters' tax-deduction bill, and sure enough, there was another waterway user charge bill. "Transportation Users Equity Act of 1979," it was called, and it proposed that the government impose a user charge based on the annual federal cost of waterway-construction projects. The sponsor was Berkley Bedell. "I don't think we can give up on this issue," Bedell said, softly but firmly, a few days after he introduced the measure. "That bill we passed last year still doesn't give you any real connection between the government's cost and the fee the barges pay. Berk Bedell's not going to give up on this until we get a barge fee that makes some sense."

On the Senate side, however, there was no waterway bill. "I'm not going to get into that fight again," Pete Domenici said. "I think we did pretty well last year—hell, the odds were 90 to 1 we wouldn't get any user charge at all." Domenici, clearly, was still savoring the memory of his victory. "Look, it was fun to win," he said. "It is the

Index